Excel Can Do That!?

Real-world Examples that Allow You to Start Writing
VBA Excel Code in Minutes

By Jim Boston and Louis Janis

Copyright © 2010

Thank you
to Joanne and Rosemary
for putting up with us

Introduction

The goal of this book is to allow students, teachers, technicians, engineers, hobbyists, and others with an interest in using Microsoft's Excel to do interesting and useful tasks not standard to the Excel toolkit. We will do this by showing you how to use an accessible programming language called Visual Basic for Applications (VBA). VBA is simply Visual Basic, which is already built into many Microsoft Office programs, such as Word, PowerPoint, Access, and Excel.

This book is not meant for professional, full-time programmers or computer science majors. While these audiences will find many useful examples and material in this book, this book is not intended to be rigorous enough to provide the level of theoretical insight they require for accreditation in their endeavors. What this book does aim to do is to allow people either forced, or just inclined, to deal with Microsoft Excel at the VBA level, and to provide them with near-term ability and knowledge to quickly become productive in the production of Excel VBA applications.

There are two ways to use VBA in Excel. One way to get started is simply to place controls onto a spreadsheet. This is shown in the sections about Toolbar Controls and adding sound and video of this text. This method requires only the writing of the code that is to be executed when the control is clicked on or in response to some other event. The other way is to set up a project with modules in addition to writing code. We have organized the code examples in this book into six modules that use this project approach. A description of the project method follows.

Many of the examples in this book are geared toward people dealing with systems integration projects, but they can be used for many applications. Many have pointed out that life itself is a project , and thus, many of the examples demonstrated here can be applied toward requirements you face in your life.

The examples in this book are broken up into a project with six modules and a section covering sound and video:

Module 1 -- Definitions
Module 2 -- Manipulating an Excel Workbook
Module 3 -- Producing Drawings
Module 4 -- Handling Finances
Module 5 -- Project Planning
Module 6 -- Generating Simple Floor Plans
Module 7 – Pizzaz – Audio or Video

The first section of the book will cover basic information required to write, modify, and debug VBA code. You will quickly learn how to get around the VBA project environment, how to start writing simple programs by recording macros, and how to create command buttons. From there, you will learn how to create VBA software structures and how to use VBA to manipulate Microsoft Excel worksheets. Finally, you will learn how to troubleshoot problems with VBA code.

After this initial VBA introduction section we will move into the various examples mentioned above in the order listed. We will show you how to automatically generate worksheets, how to hide and unhide worksheets, and how to generate and manipulate toolbars to create easy-to-use shortcuts to programs you create.

Next we will show you how to make Excel act as a drawing program to create simple objects and lines. We will then show you how to make Excel create complex lines, blocks, and other objects.

In the next section we will demonstrate how VBA can be used to calculate finances, totally outside of the formulas that can be built into cells.

The remainder of this book will show how to use Excel to plan, design, and implement various aspects of a program. But, first, we need to introduce how we get Excel to automate many tasks. We will even show you how Excel can mimic many of the 2D features of mechanical drawing software.

Download Companion Spreadsheet

You can download a workbook that corresponds to the examples in this book at:

www.vindicom.com

Getting Started with VBA

Now let's get back to the actual implementation of code. Visual Basic for Applications (VBA) is built into most Microsoft Office applications. It is considered event-driven software because events drive the operation of the software. The VBA code provided is a collection of functions or macros that react to user input and data it encounters, usually the result of the contents of cells in worksheets. This software does not rely on formulas loaded into cells; it is all executed from VBA functions (macros).

An Integrated Development Environment, also known as an IDE, is provided as part of VBA in Excel. The IDE provides project panels showing files included in the project-- forms, properties, code, and a symbolic debugger. The VBA IDE can be opened in one of three ways:

a) Click on the VBA icon 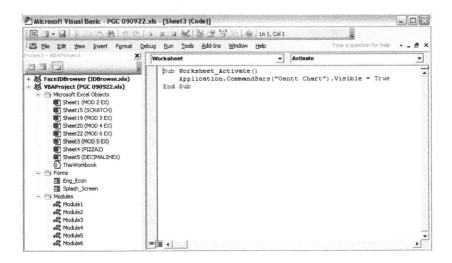 on the VBA toolbar (if it is selected via View->Toolbars-> Visual Basic)
b) Press Alt+F11; or
c) Click on Tools -> Macros -> Visual Basic Editor

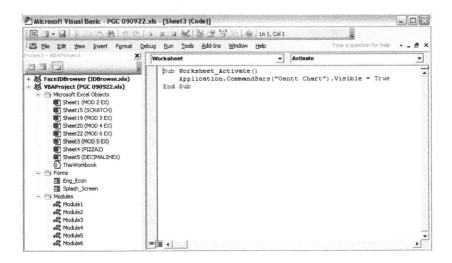

Visual Basic Editor

The navigation window on the left lists all worksheets, user forms, or code modules.

The window on the right shows the selected object. Each worksheet, user form, and code module is considered an Excel object.

The Workbook Object

This object is at the bottom of the list of worksheet objects. The Workbook object is the code module for the entire workbook. Whatever code is put into this module is run at program startup. The code for this module can be found in the Source Code listing. We use the Workbook to assign a few functions to Alt keys and to show the opening Splash page.

Notice that the functions contain numerous Boolean functions set either true or false. If a function was running and called up a worksheet that would normally open a form, that event would stop the function until the form was manually closed. To prevent that from happening, Boolean functions associated with most forms are set at the start of a function to prevent a form from opening, and then reset at the end of the function to allow the form to reopen when needed.

Let's Begin

The workbook opens up on the Module 2 Examples (MOD 2 EX) worksheet. When the program first starts up, the Project toolbar is also opened.

Selecting a number opens the worksheet associated with that module. The arrow down symbol closes or hides all the sheets except the MOD 2 and the SCRATCH sheets.

It can be hidden and later recalled by selecting
View -> Toolbars -> Projects.

The software is broken up into modules in the Visual Basic section of the workbook. Each module corresponds to code listed in the examples section listed above. We used Module 1 to declare all public variables.

Note: You will find that the first time you record a macro after Excel has started that Excel will create a new code module. If you record a macro of your own, a seventh module will be added to the six modules we provided. You can easily cut and paste code from one module to another and delete unwanted modules by right clicking on the module to be eliminated.

What VBA can do with Excel

VBA is used to take a macro and turn it into a function that can automate the operation of Excel. It can be used to eliminate any repetitive tasks, especially those prone to mistakes. These can include tasks such as making sure bills are paid on time and ensuring that parts are not used twice or a bill is not paid twice.

A little Software Background

VBA takes many of the original features of BASIC and expands on them. Long gone is the need for line numbers as in the old BASIC. VBA has adopted some of the features of other more powerful languages, such as Select Case statements from the C family. Using VBA also generally allows for quicker development time. VBA code runs more slowly than C++ and others; but, for what this book covers, speed won't be an issue. VBA is a subset of VB (Visual Basic) and their properties, methods, and events are fairly close but not identical. But for the command syntax (For/Next; Select Case, Format(), etc.), VBA is a direct subset of VB. For .com objects--that is, the actual communications between VBA/VB) and various Microsoft Office objects, every version of VBA has its unique hierarchy. This means you can't export a VBA program from Excel to Word, Access, or Visio and expect it to work, as each program has a different set of objects. You can import VBA forms into VB at the price of a longer runtime, but most VB forms cannot be imported into VBA, although VB .com components can be imported into VBA projects.

While many professional software developers prefer C++ to VBA, VBA is probably the optimal language for Excel projects and is used by engineers, scientists, and the world of finance. We envision that the people who will want to understand the code and add and enhance it will <u>not</u> have day jobs as programmers but will have other technical expertise that includes some coding ability. Because VBA is a part of the Excel file, it does not require a separate development tool, such as Microsoft Visual Studio, to create a working application. Unlike C++, C#, VB,

Java, and other languages that need to be distributed as .exe, .dll, or other file types and be compiled, VBA is free with Excel. Although other languages need the ability to write to the OS registry to let Excel know an add-in exists, the VBA code is part of the Excel file. Notification to the operating system is not required. VBA may also access .com add-ins. These .com files may be added into your Excel VBA program by pointing and clicking, or at most, entering a single line of code. Our examples provide any references needed to run the provided code.

Although we refer to a sequence of instructions as procedures, there are two different code types: functions and subroutines. Both a function and a subroutine accept parameters from the calling procedure; only the function returns a parameter to the calling procedure. Procedures are generally stand-alone code segments, while functions and subroutines often are interconnected. In VBA the term subroutine, abbreviated Sub and End Sub, is used to create a block of code that is executed line by line when an event happens or it is called by another part of the code.

Procedures, subroutines, and functions may be recursive, that is, they may call themselves. We have tried to avoid this because each call to itself requires that the current state of the procedure is pushed onto the stack, and hence might result in a stack overflow and cause Excel to crash.

Subroutines or functions take a few different constructs. The Sequence construct is the simplest, because statements are executed in the order they're found in the code.

The advantage of using a subroutine or function is that it eliminates the need to type a common task into many places in the code. Any changes are only made in the subroutine or function and not in many places in the code. This lessens the likelihood that you'll overlook changes in the code and have to go back later and debug the code again when an unchanged subroutine results in an undesired behavior.

The other two are the Selection and Iteration constructs, both of which require a logical test of some sort. (An If/Then or Select Case statement is a logical test.) Logical tests can be performed on variables, calculations, results of functions, and controls (buttons, checkboxes, etc.). The test will result in true, false, or null/empty values. The Selection constructs are used when the flow of execution may flow down two or more paths.

The Iteration constructs are used when a block of code is required to be executed continually until a condition is met (such as a Do loop). Sometimes the numbers of iterations required are known in advance. In these cases a counted loop may be used (such as a For/Next statement).

We cover the various constructs a little more closely soon. Before going onto programming it is necessary to set the security levels of your PC to allow VBA code and macros to run.

Security

Security settings in the operating system may prevent you from developing or running VBA code. To prevent malicious software from harming your computer or stealing your identity run software only from trusted sources. To set security at a level that will allow your VBA code to run, in Excel go to Tools, Macro, and Security as shown below.

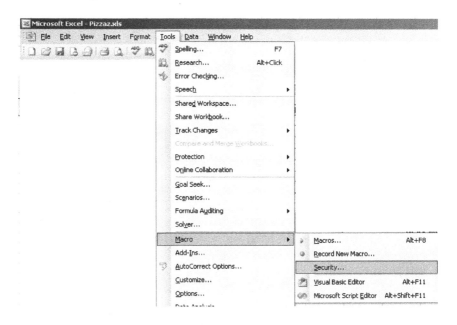

Click on security and the following form will appear.

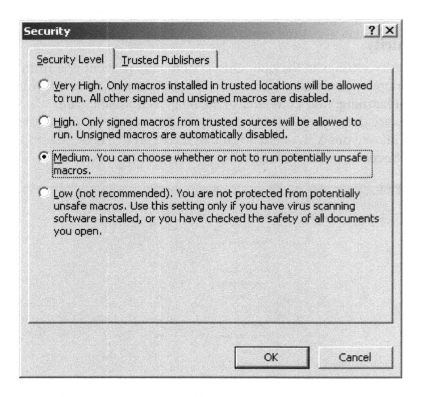

Select Medium or Low to allow your VBA code to run. If you choose Medium, you will be asked if you want to run specific VBA code. If you choose Low, you will not be asked if a specific VBA code should run, it will be allowed in all cases. Because macros are implemented in VBA code, the security warning asks if you wish to enable macros or disable macros. To allow you to run your VBA code select Enable Macros. You must close the Excel program and reopen it for these changes to take effect.

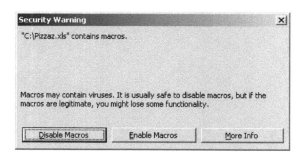

Finding Files

Later portions of this text will require the ability to find files on your computer to use in the examples. This is also a good skill to have in working with your programs, projects, and work in general. To find a given type of file if you know its extension, use the *Search for Files* capability in any of the Microsoft Windows operating systems. In this example we're searching for a wave file. Its extension is ".wav." First, click on *Start*, followed by *Search* and finally *For Files or Folders* as shown below:

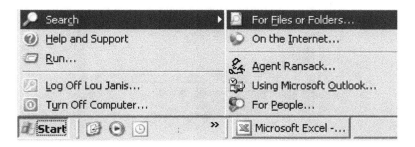

Select *All Files and Folders* from the next menu.

Next type *.wav* into the *All or part of the file name* textbox as shown.

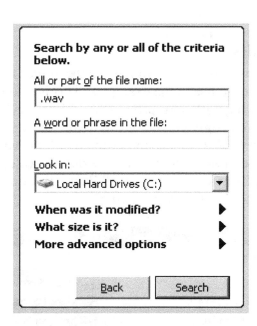

Searching in the C:\Windows directory may be a bit faster:

Name	In Folder
wmpaud9.wav	C:\WINDOWS\Help
xpstart.wav	C:\WINDOWS\Serv
xplogon.wav	C:\WINDOWS\Serv
ringin.wav	C:\WINDOWS\Serv
utopiaex.wav	C:\WINDOWS\Serv
xpcrtstp.wav	C:\WINDOWS\Serv
ringout.wav	C:\WINDOWS\Serv
xpshutdn.wav	C:\WINDOWS\Serv

In the section dealing with playing a wave file you will need to copy the wave file to the root directory. The file will then be referenced by a path and name. The path consists of the drive letter followed by a colon and backslash. This refers to the root of the C drive. The name then follows with an extension. For example: *C:\ringin.wav*. For playing wave or MIDI files, displaying a picture, or playing a video file, knowing the file's location on your PC is required.

17

The Excel VBA Project Environment

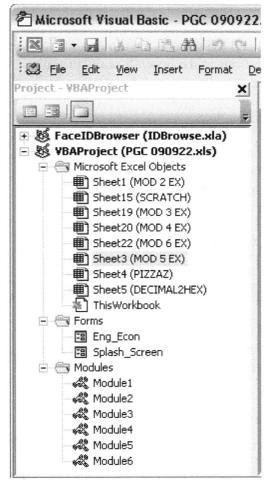

There are three types of Excel objects. These show up on the left side of Microsoft Visual Basic screen as seen to the left. These objects are worksheets (seen at the top), forms, and code modules.

Every time you record a new macro (see next section) after you have opened a workbook, a new module is added to the code modules. If you don't want to keep those extra modules you can right click on a particular module and select *Remove Module*.

To see the code associated with any workbook or code module simply double click on the desired object. If you double click on a form you will see the form in a graphics editor. To see the code associated with the form, select an object on the form and double click again.

If you happen to select an object on a form that currently has no function associated with it, a new blank function will be created when the form's code module is open. The same thing will happen if you double click an open area of the form.

A better way to see the source code associated with a form is to simply right click on the desired form label as seen on the left and select *View Code*.

We have generally organized the code in the numbered modules to correspond with the sections in the book. It really doesn't matter what module you put code into, as a function or subroutine call can be in any module and be called by another function in any other code module.

The only exception to this rule is the declaration of public variables in Module 1. They must be in Module 1 to be accessible by all functions. These public variables are also known as global variables.

By default, Visual Basic will let you watch a function as it performs its operations. This is often helpful in troubleshooting and understanding how a function works. The trade-off is some penalty in speed. In almost all instances the trade-off for what we are doing is minimal.

The command to turn off the viewing of operational updating is: *Application.ScreenUpdating = False*

Displaying the VBA Toolbar

Displaying VBA toolbar allows you to toggle among edit and run modes and the Control Toolbox, change security settings, enter the Visual Basic editor, and control macros. To display the VBA toolbar select *View, Toolbars, Visual Basic*.

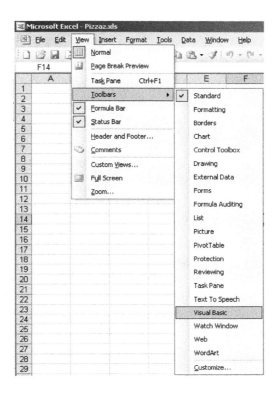

Here is the Visual Basic toolbar.

Click on the control toolbox menu bar to see the various tools available in Excel VBA.

Here is the control toolbox menu bar:

Design mode is where controls are placed onto a spreadsheet and VBA code is written. Knowing which mode you are in will prevent frustration. Look carefully at the Design mode symbols below.

 Design mode (notice the box around the icon)

Run mode (notice no box around the icon)

The *Properties* form holds the parameters for a control, such as caption, size, and visible. More on this later.

View Code allows you to open a window to view VBA code. There are other ways to view the code that you will use more often. More on this later.

All the controls shown are capable of causing an event. An event is when the operating system detects a user interaction with a control. Clicking, double clicking, or hovering a mouse or other pointing device while it is over a control will generate an event. The event will cause the code associated with that control to execute. The execution of the code only happens if there is code written in the subroutine for that control and that specific event. For instance you can click a mouse button over a command button control and execute one subroutine, while double clicking the mouse button over a command button control would execute the code in a different subroutine. Should there be no code defined for the double click subroutine of that control, and then no action would occur. In the examples that follow the command button is used extensively.

The *More Controls* button opens a list of other controls not used as frequently as the ones shown on the Control Toolbox menu bar.

Toolbox Controls

Read the sections on Security, Displaying the VBA toolbar, and using the Command Button before going onto the other controls. The toolbar holds the toolbox and the toolbox holds various controls. Here is what a toolbox looks like. Controls provide the means to communicate from your software to the user and from the user into the software.

Command Button

The command button is an easy way for the user of your VBA code to perform an action. To perform an action, just push the command button. Many things do happen, most of which are handled by the operating system (OS). You don't need to be concerned about them. The advantage of VBA or other high-level languages is that the language and the OS take care of underlying details such as the placement of the cursor, and the location and operations of the mouse and the keyboard, so you can you can focus on getting the computer to do what you tell it to do using VBA.

First, the command button must be placed on the spreadsheet. Next, its properties must be set, and finally, you must enter the VBA code that tells the computer what is to be done when the command button is pressed.

To place a command button on the spreadsheet, left click the button icon

Move the pointer to the desired place on the spreadsheet for the button. Press and hold the left mouse button while dragging the pointer down and to the right. Finally, release the left mouse button. Here is the result.

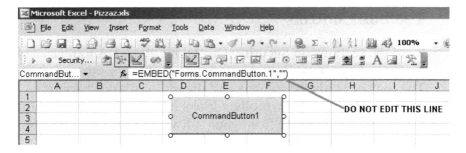

The button can be resized using the handles on the corners, top, bottom, and sides. Open the *Properties* form by right clicking the mouse button over the command button..

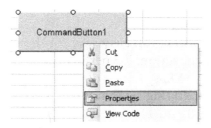

Click on *Properties* and see the following.

23

Notice the *Name* is CommandButton1 and it has no spaces between the words. The name of a command button must only contain letters, a number, and a few special characters. The *Caption* is the letters, number, and characters that show on the face of the button. Change the words associated with the *Caption* and see the change on the button. *Font* properties can also be changed, including the font, size, bold, and italic.

Lower down is the property *Visible*. Making *Visible* false will cause the button to disappear when in the *Run* mode. In *Design* mode all controls are visible; only in *Run* mode will they become invisible if *Visible* is set to false.

After changing the *Caption* to My Button, we close the *Properties* form.

Double clicking the left mouse button will open the VBA code form and allow you to enter your VBA code.

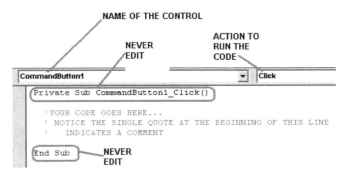

Many other actions are available to run this code. *Click* and Double Click (*DblClick*) are the most common.

24

Checkbox

To create a checkbox, click the *Checkbox* icon in the *Toolbox Controls*, move the pointer onto the spreadsheet, left click and hold to begin the corner of the checkbox, and continue to hold the left mouse button down while dragging it to the desired point on the lower right, where it is released. To access the properties of the checkbox, double click it to access a drop-down menu and left click once to open the *Properties* form (is that right?)

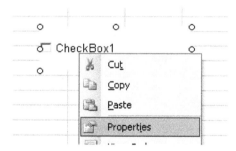

The two properties you will need are *Caption* and *Value*. The name of the checkbox may be changed from the default of CheckBox1 to any other unused name consisting of letters and numbers without any spaces and beginning with a letter. The property may be set in the *Properties* form and changed as needed by your software. The check may be checked or unchecked by the user or the software.

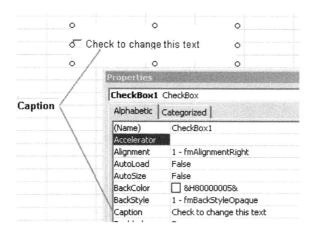

The value property being true displays a check in the box.

☑ Check to change this text

The value property being false displays an empty box.

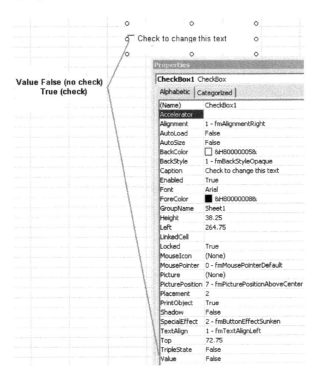

Here is a program to change the caption of the checkbox depending on whether the user checks or unchecks the box. To enter the code, double click the left pointer button.

```
Private Sub CheckBox1_Click()

    'check box responds to a change in the box
    If CheckBox1.Value = True Then
        CheckBox1.Caption = "This box is checked"        'the box has been checked by the user
    Else
        CheckBox1.Caption = "This box is not checked"    'the box has been unchecked by the user
    End If

End Sub
```

You are allowed to place as many checkboxes on a spreadsheet as you desire, and each one works independently of the others. This means they may all be checked, some may be checked, or none may be checked at any given time. Option buttons work differently from checkboxes.

Option Button

The option button is sometimes called a radio button. The option button works the same way the select station's button works on your radio. You can only select one station to listen to at a given time. The same is true with the option button; only one may be selected at any given time. Selecting one will deselect the others. It is also possible for all option buttons to be deselected at the same time.   Place two option buttons on a spreadsheet and watch this work. In multiple-sheet applications the option buttons on different sheets do not interfere with each other.

27

The three option button properties used most often are *Name*, *Caption*, and *Value*. *Name* and *Caption* work the same for option buttons as for command buttons and checkboxes. The *Value* is true for selected and false for not selected.

```
Private Sub OptionButton1_Click()

        OptionButton1.Caption = "It's me! "
        OptionButton2.Caption = "Not me.. "

End Sub

Private Sub OptionButton2_Click()

        OptionButton2.Caption = "It's me! "
        OptionButton1.Caption = "Not me.. "

End Sub
```

Notice the number of the option button changes in each subroutine from line to line.

Textbox

The textbox is selected and inserted into the spreadsheet in the same way as a command button or a checkbox. Access to properties is accomplished in the same way for all the controls. The textbox allows the user to enter words, numbers, or special characters to be processed by the software. It also allows the software to display messages for the user. These messages may be any visible character: numbers, letters, or special characters, (.,!@#$%^&*(){}[]:"';).

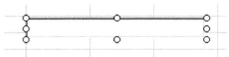

The basic properties of the textbox are *Name, Text,* and
MultiLine. These three properties are a good place to start, but
the ability to change *BackColor, ForeColor,* and *Font,* and add
scrollbars adds flexibility and allows much more useful
programs.

Scrollbars are available in textboxes as you add more text. If the
text no longer fits the size of the textbox, a scrollbar appears if
the property is selected.

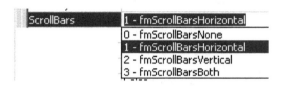

Notice that *fmScrollBarHorizontal* is selected from the
Properties drop-down box. The box shown below is empty
when created in *Design* mode. Go to *Run* mode and type enough
characters to fill the box horizontally and the scrollbar appears.
Add more characters and the scrollbar slider becomes smaller as
the displayed part of the code becomes a smaller part of all the
typed characters.

If you want to scroll vertically you will have to set the property
multiline to True and then select the *fmScrollBarsVertical* setting
in the *Scrollbars* property.

Here is a program that will convert a Y typed by the user into the
word Yes. Typing anything except Y will clear the textbox.

```
Private Sub TextBox1_Change()

    If TextBox1.Text = "Y" Or TextBox1.Text = "YES" Then
        TextBox1.Text = "YES"      ' keep YES or convert the Y to YES
    Else
        TextBox1.Text = ""          ' empty the textbox
    End If

End Sub
```

Notice if you type Textbox1, the following drop-down box appears showing the many properties you can choose related to a textbox. This feature is available for all the controls.

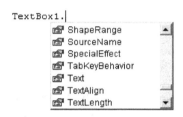

Label A

The label is a string of text that may be placed on the spreadsheet and modified by software. The user of your software is not allowed to modify a label's caption, but user events such as click and others apply to a label. The two most used properties of a label are the *Name* and the *Caption*.

Here is some code to demonstrate single- and double-click events on a label.

```
Private Sub Label1_Click()

    Label1.Caption = "I've been clicked on!"    ' single click on left pointing device button

End Sub

Private Sub Label1_DblClick(ByVal Cancel As MSForms.ReturnBoolean)

    Label1.Caption = "I've been double clicked on!"    ' double click on left pointing device button

End Sub
```

The way to select what type of event--click, double click, or others--is going to run your code is to select it when you are in the *Code* window. An example of the code window is shown below:

Notice that double click (*DblClick*) is selected for the "I've been double clicked..." code and *Click* is selected for the "I've been clicked..." code. The drop-down list contains the type of event that causes the code to execute. The operating system takes care of all the details.

Toggle button

The toggle button remembers whether it was clicked on (or other action) or not, similar to a light switch. When you use a light switch, it remembers the state of being "on" until you move the lever to "off," and then it stays off until turned back on. This is how the toggle button works. The *Value* property remains true until the toggle button is clicked or another action causes it to become false. This is different from the command button, which is like a pushbutton and acts only when clicked or another action is performed.

The code below illustrates the operation of the toggle button.

```
Private Sub ToggleButton1_Click()

    If ToggleButton1.Value = True Then
        ToggleButton1.Caption = "I'm PUSHED"
    Else
        ToggleButton1.Caption = "I'm RELEASED"
    End If

End Sub
```

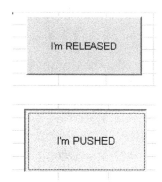

You could change the caption to display On when the value is true and Off when the value is false.

Scrollbar

You have seen scrollbars in Windows forms that are larger than your display. Scrollbars are also used in textboxes. A scrollbar may be vertical, horizontal, or both. These scrollbars allow you to position the viewable information in the display making it visible. Scrollbars may also be used to enter a value. Similar to a slider volume control, the position of the slider determines the volume of the sound from a radio or your computer.

The code below increases the height of a *Scrollbar* control as the slider is moved left to right and released and decreases the height of the *Scrollbar* control as the slider is moved from right to left and released.

```
Private Sub ScrollBar1_Change()

    ScrollBar1.Max = 200
    ScrollBar1.Min = 20
    ScrollBar1.SmallChange = 5
    ScrollBar1.Height = ScrollBar1.Value

End Sub
```

When using a scrollbar, the maximum value produced is specified by *ScrollBar1.Max*, the minimum value produced is specified by *ScrollBar1.Min*, and the size of the steps between maximum and minimum is specified by *ScrollBar1.SmallChange*. You can change the height of the control by setting the *ScrollBar1.Height* equal to the current value of the scrollbar.

The scrollbar is shown below with minimum, middle, and maximum positions of the slider marked.

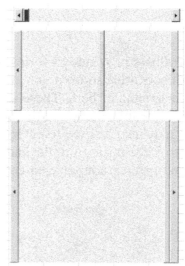

As you can see, the height changes with the slider position. Because you can control the height by the slider position, you can also use a different control to obtain a value, and then use that value to position the slider. The simplest case would look like this:

ScrollBar1.Value = OtherControl.Value

Spin button

The spin button is similar to the scrollbar in that it increases and decreases a value. The spin button, also called a spinner, only modifies a value. The value can be made visible using a textbox or other control. It can also be used in a calculation. The range of values are defined using either the properties form or under program control.

```
' set the range
SpinButton1.Min = 1          ' set the minimum value
SpinButton1.Max = 10         ' set the maximum value
' set the current value
SpinButton1.Value = 5        ' this can be anywhere in the range
```

Also the orientation of the spin button may selected using the properties form or by program control. Here is a short program to increase or decrease a value displayed in a textbox followed by the properties form.

```
Private Sub SpinButton1_Change()

    TextBox3.Text = SpinButton1.Value

End Sub
```

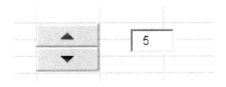

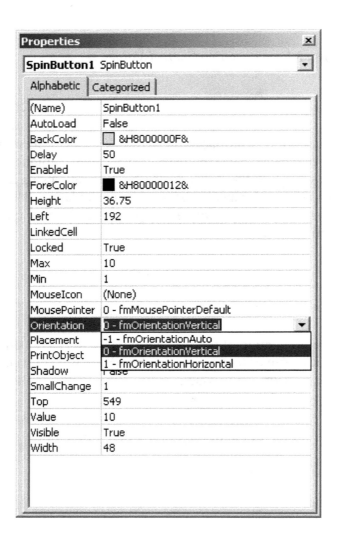

Combo box

The combo box allows selection of one item from a list of items. First we must generate the list of items, and then we can use the combo box to select one of them. The items may be entered using program control using AddItem, setting the list property, or referencing cells on the spreadsheet. This example references cells on the spreadsheet.

First type the items into cells, one item per cell. Next, place the combo box and a textbox to display the selection, and finally, set the following properties in the properties form. (Many properties are not shown; accept the defaults for these properties.)

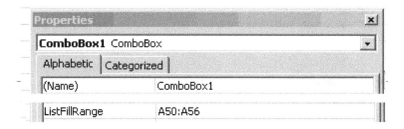

The *ListFillRange* property provides the link from the combo box to the cells holding the items. The code to combine a message the selection and place the result in a textbox is shown below

```
Private Sub ComboBox1_Change()

    TextBox4.Text = "The selected day is " + ComboBox1.Text 'a message goes into a Text Box

End Sub
```

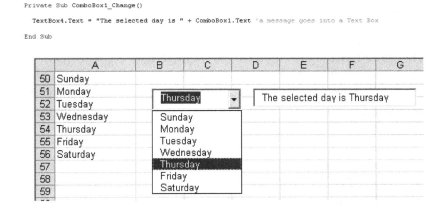

Creating a list of items using *AddItem* would be as follows using a command button.

36

```
Private Sub CommandButton1_Click()

    'Clear and place the items into the ComboBox2
    ComboBox2.Clear
    ComboBox2.AddItem "One"
    ComboBox2.AddItem "Two"
    ComboBox2.AddItem "Three"
    ComboBox2.AddItem "Four"
    ComboBox2.AddItem "Five"
    ComboBox2.AddItem "Six"

End Sub
```

The combination of the command button and combo box are shown below:

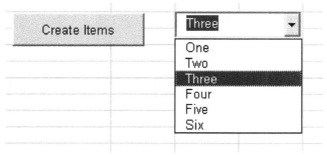

The three most useful methods to manage lists are *AddItem*, *Clear*, and *RemoveItem*. *AddItem* is used to add an item to a list. Clear is used to empty the list. Removeitem is used to delete an item from the list. An index is also provided to reference items in the list.

There are many properties not described here and other ways of populating lists. As you find the need to extend your skills, be sure to look into lists, arrays, sorting, and of course, the extensive properties of all the controls.

37

List box

The list box is similar to the combo box. The combo box drops down to show items for selection; the list box shows the whole list or allows you to scroll up and down using arrows if the number of selections is greater than the size of the box.

Notice the example below is very similar to the one for the combo box, but the box does not drop down.

First, fill the items using the command button and *AddItem*; second, place the list box and textbox on the form and size them for the expected strings. Finally, link the changes in the list box to the textbox as shown in the code that follows.

```
Private Sub CommandButton2_Click()

    'Clear and place the items into the ListBox1
    ListBox1.Clear
    ListBox1.AddItem "Sue"
    ListBox1.AddItem "Sam"
    ListBox1.AddItem "Adam"

End Sub

Private Sub ListBox1_Click()

    TextBox5.Text = ListBox1.Text  'place the name into the TextBox

End Sub
```

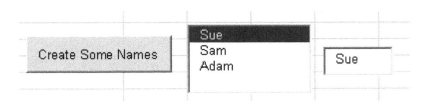

When the name Sue is selected, the click event occurs in the list box and the name is displayed in the textbox.

38

Macros – An Easy Way to Start Programming

Recording a macro is the easiest way to discover the commands for controlling Excel (or any of the other Office products) outside of Visual Basic. A macro is a set or list of instructions that performs a task or set of tasks. Excel allows you to record a macro that converts a series of mouse and keyboard commands that you enter into a corresponding set of instructions that Excel understands. You can record a macro in two different ways. If you have the Visual Basic toolbar viewable (View -> Toolbars -> Visual Basic) then just select the red dot to start recording.

The second way is to select Tools -> Macros -> Record New Macro.

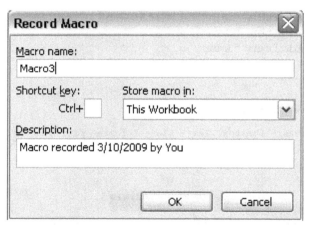

This GUI appears. Name the macro and add any description you like.

This form also lets you add a shortcut key so you can run the macro by pressing the Control (Ctrl) key plus the shortcut key.

Another way you can run your macro is by selecting Tools -> Macros -> (Select desired macro) Run.

We will refer to a piece of code as a macro if it only contains Excel commands and no VBA. If the code contains both, we will refer to it as a function (remembering that a true function has external variables handed to it, while a procedure is a true stand-alone piece of VBA code).

Another way to run a macro (functions and macros are interchangeable in these GUIs) is to select *Edit* instead of *Run* and, with the cursor anywhere in the macro/function you want to run, press F5. Or, you can go manually into the code module of the macro/function you want to run and, with the cursor anywhere within the macro/function, press F5.

Here is the result of a recorded macro in which all that is done is to select cell E22.
As in many languages, an apostrophe at the start of any line means that the line that follows is a comment and is not interpreted as code. Macros/functions all start with Sub "Name" and end with End Sub.

Sub MyFirstMacro( )
' Macro recorded 3/10/2010 by You
    Range("E22").Select
End Sub

There's no Visual Basic code here, just an Excel command to select a cell.

The GUI below shows how you select a macro or function to edit or to run.

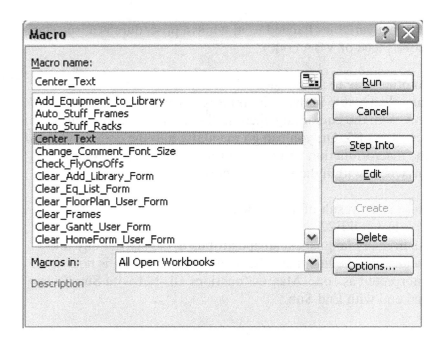

Tools->Macros->
gets you to this GUI.

Select macro (they are list alphabetically) and select *Run* or *Edit*.

If *Edit* is selected you are taken to the code module that the selected macro is in and to the start of that macro.

If you write a new function inside a code module, as opposed to recording a macro, it also appears in the above list with the recoded macros. Functions you write and macros you record are the same for all intents and purposes.

Below is a screenshot of the VBA Project Environment GUI. Excel objects are on the left. If you look closely you can see that code module 9 is selected and a function is shown. In the upper-right corner a drop-down box allows you to select any function/macro in that code module. Functions/macros are listed in alphabetical order.

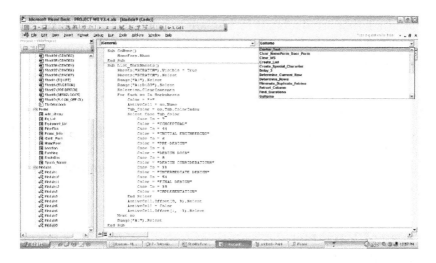

Declaring Variables (Module 1)

Variables are used for temporary storage of numbers and strings. The variable name is simply an identifier used to label the data. In VB, variables must begin with a letter and must be less than 255 characters in length. VB doesn't require a variable to be declared before use--we could simply declare in the middle of a function that x = 2 or y = ActiveCell, or Fred = x + 3, etc. However, this is definitely not recommended. Although we haven't done it here, we could specify Option Explicit by selecting Tools -> Options -> Editor tab and checking the *Require Variable Declaration* box, which would require you to declare all variables before they are first used.

As a general rule, it is best to declare variables at the beginning of the code. Several possible ways of declaring a variable exist, and the way we declare a variable determines its scope and duration.

If we use *Dim* before a variable in a function it means that this variable is only used and available to this function. If variables are defined at the top of a module they are available to all functions in that module. The default setting for an *Integer* value is zero and the default setting for a *String* is set to empty, etc..

Variables that are declared *Public* are available to all functions in all modules. Although it is stated that Public variables can be declared in any module, we have found that to reduce confusion it is best to declare a variable Public in Module 1. As you will see in the section on Public variables below, they have all been declared in Module 1.

Variables that need to hold their value between calls are declared as *Static*. A variable declared as *Const* (constant) is a special form of variable with a value that does not change throughout the program.

Types of Variables

The *As* that follows each variable is required to set the variable type. If the *As* is omitted, the variable is automatically defined as a *Variant*.

Byte: Integer of 8-bit value, thus has a value between 0 and 255
Boolean: Single bit value that is either True or False
Integer: Integer of 16-bit value, value from -32768 to +32767 (whole numbers only)
Long: Integer of 32-bit value from (-2,147,483,648 to +2,147,483,647) (why aren't these two numbers the same?)
Currency: Values from the +/- 922 trillion range
Single: Single-precision, 32-bit (eight significant digits) floating-point number
Double: Double-precision, 64-bit (16 significant digits) floating-point number
Date: Date value
String: Holds up to a 63,000-character sequence
Variant: Type that will change based on the value that is assigned to the variable

Navigating around a workbook
Navigation around a workbook using macros/functions/procedures doesn't require VBA. . It simply requires knowing the set of commands that Excel will respond to get you where you need to go. If you want variables to help decide where exactly you want to go, then it takes some VBA.

Below is a list of commands and what they do. First we will show you how to perform actions without VBA, then using VBA.

Open a workbook:
Workbooks.Open Filename:="*c:\"Path"\"target excel file*"

With VBA
Sub open_workbook()
    Dim workbook_name As String
    Dim path As String
    workbook_name = "Project"
    Path = "c:\My Documents\New Project\"
    Workbooks.Open Filename:= Path & workbook_name &
".xls"
End Sub

To select a different workbook:
Workbooks("desired_workbook").Activate

With VBA
Sub open_different_workbook()
    Dim workbook_name As String
    workbook_name = "Project"
    Workbooks(workbook_name).Activate
End Sub

To select a particular worksheet in a workbook:
Sheets("desired_worksheet").Select

With VBA
Sub open_different_worksheet()
    Dim worksheet_name As String
    worksheet_name = "RACK ELEVATION"
    Sheets (worksheet_name).Select
End Sub

To select a particular column on a worksheet:
Columns("BM:BM").Select

With VBA
Sub select_a_column( )
Dim column_selected As String
column_selected = "BM"
Columns(column_selected & ":" &
column_selected).Select
End Sub

To select a particular row in worksheet:
Rows("17:17").Select

With VBA
Sub select_a_row( )
Dim row_selected As Integer
row_selected = 17
Rows(row_selected & ":" & row_selected).Select
End Sub

To select a particular cell in a worksheet:
Range("C5").Select

With VBA
Sub select_a_cell( )
Dim cell_selected As String
cell_selected = "C5"
Range(cell_selected).Select
End Sub

To move from one cell to another:
ActiveCell.Offset(3, 5).Select
(move down three rows and over five columns)

With VBA
Sub select_a_different_cell( )
Dim different_row As Integer
Dim different_column As Integer
different_row = 3
different_column = 5
ActiveCell.Offset(different_row, different_column).Select

End Sub

To remember a point to come back to:
Point = ActiveWindow.RangeSelection.Address

With VBA to get back to that point
Sub Get_Back_to_Point( )
     Range(Point).Select
End Sub

Color Coding

Excel allows you to create macros that let you change the color of whole cells or just the text within cells.

To change the color of a whole cell, such as **to** **the Excel command is:**
Selection.Interior.ColorIndex = 4

To set a worksheet's tab color, the command is:
Sheets("Worksheet Name").Tab.ColorIndex = 4

To change the color of the text inside a cell:
Selection.Font.ColorIndex = 4

In the three examples shown , the three objects--cell, tab, and font--all are turned green.

List of common ColorIndex numbers:

Formatting

With a macro we can set any properties for a cell or group of cells that we are able to set manually via Format -> Cells in the Excel main toolbar shown below:

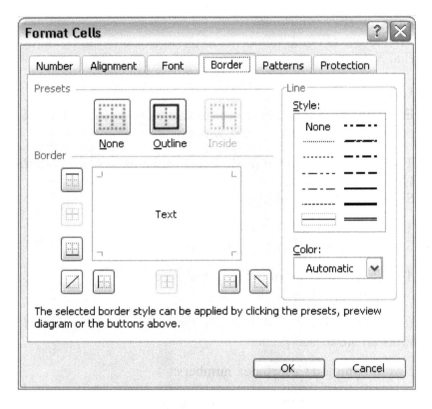

A number of tabs allow you to set cell type (*Number*), *Text Alignment*, *Font*, *Border* (the tab that is selected here), *Patterns* (cell colors), and *Cell Protection*. The *Border* tab is central to the graphical functions in Excel. It is with borders that we create boxes and lines and all the other graphic elements in Excel. As you become more familiar with the code you will see how we do this.

If we record a macro while formatting a cell we will get commands like those below.

Setting values in the *Number* tab:
Command to explicitly set a cell for Text:
Selection.NumberFormat = "@"
Number: *Selection.NumberFormat = "0.00"*
Currency: *Selection.NumberFormat = "$#,##0.00"*
Date: *Selection.NumberFormat = "m/d/yyyy"*
Time: *Selection.NumberFormat = "[$-F400]h:mm:ss AM/PM"*
Percentage: *Selection.NumberFormat = "0.00%"*
Fraction: *Selection.NumberFormat = "# ?/?"*

Setting values in the Alignment tab:
We can set several parameters at once with the *With Selection* term, and end the selection with *End With*. The terms are easily aligned with the parameters you actually find in that tab.

> *With Selection*
>   *.HorizontalAlignment = xlLeft*
>   *.VerticalAlignment = xlTop*
>   *.WrapText = True*
>   *.Orientation = 0*
>   *.AddIndent = False*
>   *.IndentLevel = 0*
>   *.ShrinkToFit = False*
>   *.ReadingOrder = xlContext*
>   *.MergeCells = False*
> *End With*

In the example shown above, if you only wanted to set whether to wrap the text:
Selection.WrapText = True
The same format would be used for any particular parameter.

Setting values in the Font tab:
Below we have set several font values, including a font color of red (ColorIndex = 3) in the selected area .

> *With Selection.Font*

```
        .Name = "Times New Roman"
        .FontStyle = "Bold"
        .Size = 12
        .Strikethrough = False
        .Superscript = False
        .Subscript = False
        .OutlineFont = False
        .Shadow = False
        .Underline = xlUnderlineStyleNone
        .ColorIndex = 3
    End With
```

From the example above to set only the font would be:
Selection.Font.Name = "Times New Roman"
Or to set only the font size.
Selection.Font.Size = 12

Setting values in the *Border* tab:
As we mentioned at the beginning of this section, this tab is
central to all the graphics we create with Excel.

In this example, we have set a thin, continuous border around a
cell or cells, depending on the area specified before these
commands.

The first two lines indicate that no diagonal lines are to be in the
area selected. The next four With/End With statements show that
left, top, bottom, and right sides of the area will have continuous
thin borders.

```
Selection.Borders(xlDiagonalDown).LineStyle = xlNone
    Selection.Borders(xlDiagonalUp).LineStyle = xlNone
    With Selection.Borders(xlEdgeLeft)
        .LineStyle = xlContinuous
        .Weight = xlThin
        .ColorIndex = xlAutomatic
    End With
    With Selection.Borders(xlEdgeTop)
        .LineStyle = xlContinuous
```

```
.Weight = xlThin
.ColorIndex = xlAutomatic
End With
With Selection.Borders(xlEdgeBottom)
.LineStyle = xlContinuous
.Weight = xlThin
.ColorIndex = xlAutomatic
End With
With Selection.Borders(xlEdgeRight)
.LineStyle = xlContinuous
.Weight = xlThin
.ColorIndex = xlAutomatic
End With
```

If you only wanted to change a single side, say the right side, to a thick line, without changing anything else, you would use the command:

Selection.Borders(xlEdgeRight) .Weight = xlThick

Setting values in the Pattern tab:
 We do this quite often: We set cells to a certain color and then come back and check the color of a cell to determine the condition associated with that cell.

```
With Selection.Interior
.ColorIndex = 4
.Pattern = xlSolid
.PatternColorIndex = xlAutomatic
End With
```

General worksheet formatting:
Often we want to set a whole worksheet or area on a worksheet to some parameter.
If you want to set a parameter for all the cells on a worksheet:
Cells.Select
If you want to select a single column: Columns("C").Select
If you want to select a number of adjacent columns:
Columns("C:F").Select
If you want to select a number of non-adjacent columns:
        Range("A:A,D:D,G:G,J:J,M:M").Select

The same can be done with rows:

Rows("36:36").Select

If you want to select an area:

Range("R2:AB11").Select

If you want to insert a column and shift everything right:

Columns("G:G").Select
Selection.Insert Shift:=xlToRight

To set column width:

Selection.ColumnWidth = 25

To delete multiple columns and shift everything to the left

Columns("G:Z").Select
Selection.Delete Shift:=xlToLeft

Again, you need to know the Excel command to accomplish something:

To find an unknown command, record a macro while performing the operation you want to automate! Viewing the macro code will reveal the desired command

Making Decisions

Earlier we talked about Selection and Iteration constructs. One of the powerful ways that VBA, or any high-level programming language, can automate a process is its ability to check the status of various things and act accordingly. The most common and best known method is the If/Then statement. It does exactly what it implies: If something happens or is true, then the software does something else.

If ActiveCell > "" Then
'Do some stuff
End if

The example above simply states that if the current cell is not empty (or, to be more exact is more than empty), then do some stuff.

If Selection.Font.ColorIndex = 4 Then

51

> *'React to cell (or area selected) being green*
> *Else:*
> *'React to cell not being green*
> *End if*

The example above is another of our favorite green-cell examples.

> *If Selection.Borders(xlDiagonalUp).Weight = xlMedium*
> *Then*
>> *Count = Count + 1*
> *End if*

The code above checks to see if the current selection or cell has a medium-weight diagonal line through it. If the selection does, then the code increases the count by one.

Another Selection construct is *Select Case*. The nice thing about this construct is that it makes it easier to select among multiple choices or conditions. *Select Case* has an optional *Case Else* code that is executed if no other case match is found.

> *Select Case Tab_Color*
>> *Case Is = 7*
>>> *Color = "CONCEPTUAL"*
>> *Case Is = 44*
>>> *Color = "INITIAL ENGINEERING"*
>>> *Case Is = 6*
>>> *Color = "PRE-DESIGN"*
>> *Case Is = 4*
>>> *Color = "DESIGN DOCS"*
>> *Case Is = 8*
>>> *Color = "DESIGN CONSIDERATIONS"*
>> *Case Is = 33*
>>> *Color = "INTERMEDIATE DESIGN"*
>> *Case Is = 54*
>>> *Color = "FINAL DESIGN"*
>> *Case Is = 38*
>>> *Color = "IMPLEMENTATION"*
> *End Select*

We checked to see what the tab color is of a workbook, and assigned a color label to it based on its value.

Notice that this is an example of "structured" programming. We indent lines based on where they reside in the hierarchy of a programming structure. Notice the indentation if we nest an *If* statement within another *If* statement.

> *If Mid(Boundary, i, 1) = "," Then*
>   *x = 2*
>   *Point_2 = Left(Boundary, i - 1)*
>   *Point_3 = Right(Boundary, Len (Boundary) - i)*
>   *If Point_3 > "" Then*
>   *x = 3*
>   *End If*
> *End If*

Here we are looking for a comma in the middle of a string called *Boundry*. If we find it, we drop everything in Boundry before that character and call what is left *Point_3*. If *Point_3* still has something left in the string, we set x = 3.

See how the second, or nested, *If/Then* statement is more indented than the first *If/Then* statement? This format helps us see more easily that the second *If/Then* statement resides within the first *If/Then* statement.

This structure is easier to read than:

> *If Mid(Boundry, i, 1) = "," Then*
> *x = 2*
> *Point_2 = Left(Boundry, i - 1)*
> *Point_3 = Right(Boundry, Len(Boundry) - i)*
> *If Point_3 > "" Then*
> *x = 3*
> *End If*
> *End If*

Performing an Action Repeatedly

This is also known as iteration. We often need to perform the same action over and over until some condition is satisfied, or we need to repeat an action a predetermined number of times. In the first instance we use a structure known as a *Do* loop. In the second we use a *For/Next* loop.

The basic *Do/* loop repeats a specified action until a built-in *Selection* statement ends the loop. *Do* loops have several ways to exit the loop. The first way is *Exit Do*. Its basic structure is:

> *Do*
> > *Statement*
> > *...*
> > *Statement*
> > *'Do this each time through the loop*
> > *If <the right conditions exist> Then*
> > > *Exit Do*
> > *End if*
> > *Statement*
> > *...*
> > *Statement*
> *Loop*

Another way to exit a loop is by testing a condition either prior to or after executing the statements within the *Do* loop. The name would change to *Do/Until* or *Do/While*

> *Do*
> > *'Execute these statements each time through the loop*
> > *Statement*
> > *...*
> > *Statement*
> *Loop Until (this condition is satisfied) or While (this condition is satisfied)*

Next to test before the code within the *Do* loop is executed. This time the name would be *While* loop or *Until* Loop.

> *Do While (this condition is satisfied) or Until (this condition is satisfied)*
> > '*Execute these statements each time through the loop*
> > *Statement*
> > ...
> > *Statement*
> *Loop*

Or we can stay in the loop until the *If/Then* statement is satisfied, then we can exit the *Do* loop. In this case, the statements consist of the *If/Else/End If* decision, part of which includes the *Exit Do* to terminate the looping.

> *Do*
> > *If ActiveCell > "" Then*
> > > *ActiveCell.Offset(1, 0).Select*
> > > *Row_Count = Row_Count + 1*
> > *Else:*
> > > *ActiveCell.Offset(-Row_Count, 0).Select*
> > > *Exit Do*
> > *End If*
> *Loop*

In the above example we use a Do loop to determine how many rows below a start point before we hit a blank cell. The *If/Then* statement tests that the current cell is not blank. If it isn't blank, then we go down one row to the next cell and increase the *Row_Count* by one. In the *Else* part of the statement, if the cell is blank we go back up to the start point and exit the *Do* loop. The variable *Row_Count* tells us how many rows until a blank cell is reached.

The second iterative structure is the *For/Next* loop, which repeats an action a fixed number of times. Its basic form is:

```
For i = 1 to SomeCount
    'Do this each time through the loop
Next i
```

The i value is a variable that is used to count. Because of its origins as a math variable this letter is often used. In this book we often use i, j, and k, and sometimes x, y, and z as variables.

If some desired condition is reached before we reach *SomeCount*, we could again include an *If/Then* statement with the command line *Exit For* in it to end the loop early.

In the example below, let's take the value we derived above in the *Do* loop, *Row_Count*, and do the *For/Next* loop *Row_Count* times.

```
For i = 1 To Row_Count
    If ActiveCell = Case_Selection Then
        ActiveCell.Offset(0, -3).Select
        Sheet_Name = ActiveCell
        Sheets(Sheet_Name).Visible = True
        ActiveCell.Offset(1, 3).Select
    Else:
        ActiveCell.Offset(1, 0).Select
    End If
Next i
```

Here we go down a number of rows based on *Row_Count* and with an *If/Then* statement nested inside the *For/Next* we check to see if the *ActiveCell* value is equal to a value stored in *Case_Selection*. If so, then we go left three columns and gather the name in that cell and use that name to make visible a worksheet of the same name. We then go back three cells right and one row down. If the original cell didn't equal the value *Case_Selection*, then we would simply go down one row and start the whole process over.

Below we have two *For/Next* loops, one nested within the other. This code instructs Excel to check 65 rows down (the i *For/Next*) and across 255 columns (the j *For/Next* loop [the entire width of a worksheet]). An *If/Then* with the nested *For/Next* loop checks to see if the current cell is not only not empty but that that the cell's font is also blue (*Selection.Font.ColorIndex* = 5). If we find both conditions, then we do some collection of data. In another nested *If/Then* statement we also check to see if the cell has a diagonal line inside it, and if it does, we increase count by one.

```
For i = 1 To 65
    For j = 1 To 255
        If ActiveCell > "" Then
            If Selection.Font.ColorIndex = 5 Then
                Mfgr = ActiveCell
                Point_3 =
ActiveWindow.RangeSelection.Address
                Range(Point_2).Select
                ActiveCell.Offset(1, 0).Select
                Point_2 =
ActiveWindow.RangeSelection.Address
                Range(Point_3).Select
            End If
        End If
        If
Selection.Borders(xlDiagonalUp).Weight =
xlMedium Then
            Count = Count + 1
        End If
        ActiveCell.Offset(0, 1).Select
    Next j
    ActiveCell.Offset(1, -255).Select
Next i
```

Finding Things with VBA

We can use a combination of Excel commands and VBA to parse and extract strings and data from variables and cells.

Let's start with finding a column from a point. We could find a point with the
Point = ActiveWindow.RangeSelection.Address command. It would yield a value that looked like this: Cell "C22" = C22. Now if we wanted to extract only the column ("C") value of the cell, we could use the subroutine below.

```
Sub Extract_Column()
    Point = ActiveWindow.RangeSelection.Address
    Column = Right(Point, Len(Point) - 1)
    For i = 1 To Len(Column)
      If Mid(Column, i, 1) = "$" Then
        Column = Left(Column, i - 1)
      End If
    Next i
End Sub
```

Here *Point* equals the current range or cell selected. It is in the format $<Column>$<Row>. To extract only <Column> from *Point* we first eliminate the first "$."
Column = Right(Point, Len(Point) - 1) does that. *Len(Point)* returns the number of characters that comprise the variable Point. In the case of C22, *Len(Point)* = 5. So *Right(Point, Len(Point) - 1)* means extract all the characters starting at the right (or end of *Point*) and extending Len(Point) = 5 – 1 or four characters toward the left. That would leave C$22.

Next we go through the string Column one character at a time. The *For/Next* statement does that for Len(Column) or four times. Four is new value of the truncated column.

When a $ is encountered, make Column now equal to all the characters from the left (or start) of Column up till $, but subtract the $, which leaves C. To save a little time we could have added an *Exit For* statement after Column = Left(Column, i - 1).

When we capture three points, which we will do later to create rooms and areas, or to create lines, the captured points will look like this: U59,AA63,AI66. Here we have three points at "U59," "AA63," and "AI66." We need to separate each of those three points into three separate points (yes?) and then extract each column and row from each point. We do that with a series of *Left*, *Right*, and *Mid* statements instead of *For/Next* loops.

The *For/Next* loops are generally used to step through each character in a *Point* variable looking for dollar signs, and commas, which are used to delineate parts of the *Point* for disassembly into eventual column and row values.

Creating Forms and Message Blocks

Here is a list of the current user forms as seen on the left side of the VBA Project GUI. We have created only two forms.

The *Eng_Econ* form is used in conjunction with the MOD 4 EX worksheet.
The *Splash_Screen* is seen only at startup.

Forms are used to interact with users--to prompt for input or to allow choices to be made.
As we will see shortly, forms are objects that can have their own set of functions. They can be thought of as containers for code exactly like code modules or worksheets. Forms have numerous properties that can be set for the whole form or specific objects on that form.

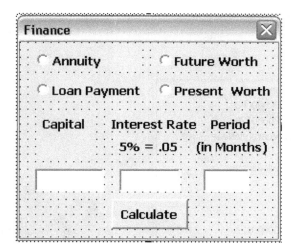

Here is the *Finance* user form. The form consists of itself and eight objects, the Annuity, Loan Payment, Future Worth, and Present Worth option buttons; the Calculate command button; and three textboxes: Capital, Interest Rate, and Period.

Following are the property dialog boxes for the form itself, and for the Calculate command button. You call up the *Property* dialog box by right clicking on the user form and then selecting the *Properties* option. It opens with the properties for the whole form. By clicking on a particular object within the user form, in this case the *Yes* button, you can view and change the properties for that object.

Properties - Eng_Econ

Eng_Econ UserForm

Alphabetic | Categorized

(Name)	Eng_Econ
BackColor	☐ &H8000000F&
BorderColor	■ &H80000012&
BorderStyle	0 - fmBorderStyleNone
Caption	Finance
Cycle	0 - fmCycleAllForms
DrawBuffer	32000
Enabled	True
Font	Tahoma
ForeColor	■ &H80000012&
Height	181.5
HelpContextID	0
KeepScrollBarsVisible	3 - fmScrollBarsBoth
Left	0
MouseIcon	(None)
MousePointer	0 - fmMousePointerDefault
Picture	(None)
PictureAlignment	2 - fmPictureAlignmentCenter
PictureSizeMode	0 - fmPictureSizeModeClip
PictureTiling	False
RightToLeft	False
ScrollBars	0 - fmScrollBarsNone
ScrollHeight	0
ScrollLeft	0
ScrollTop	0
ScrollWidth	0
ShowModal	True
SpecialEffect	0 - fmSpecialEffectFlat
StartUpPosition	1 - CenterOwner
Tag	
Top	0
WhatsThisButton	False
WhatsThisHelp	False
Width	207
Zoom	100

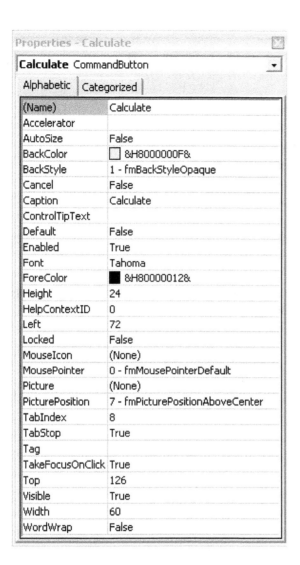

By both double clicking on an object or right clicking again and selecting the *View Code* option, you can view the code associated with the form.

Here is the code that is run when the user clicks the *Calculate* button.

```
Private Sub Calculate_Click()
    On Error GoTo Calc_Error
    Call Clear_Eng_Econ
    Cash = Eng_Econ.Cash_Amount
    Interest = Eng_Econ.Interest_Rate
    Interest2 = (Interest / 12)
    Period = Eng_Econ.Period_Mo
    Select Case Case_Selection
        Case Is = "Annuity"
            Call Calc_Annuity
        Case Is = "Future Worth"
            Call Calculate_Future_Worth
        Case Is = "Loan Payment"
            Call Calculate_Loan_Payment
        Case Is = "Present Worth"
            Call Calculate_Present_Worth
    End Select
Calc_Error:
End Sub
```

Rooting out Problems

There are two types of problems in programming. The easiest to see and usually the easiest to fix is the syntax error. This would be equivalent to a spelling error or an error in sentence structure. The second is an error in logic. Logical errors would be thinking the written code will behave a certain way, but the code behaving in an unexpected way.

For instance, there are seven days in a week. So, to determine the date of one week from today, add seven to today's date. If today's date is Monday the 3rd, then next Monday will be the 10th because 3+7 equals 10 So, you write your code accordingly. However, what if today were Monday the 27th applying the same logic, then next Monday would be the 34th because 27+7 equals 34. The code worked, but did not produce the desired results, so you would have to rethink all the cases and modify the code accordingly. Syntax errors are normally found when typing in the code or when the code is compiled. Errors in logic are normally found when the results of running the program are not as expected. Several ways to root out the problems are discussed in the following sections.

Message box

One of the simplest ways to get the user's attention during normal execution of your program or to flag a problem during a debug session is to display a message box. The simplest message box looks like this:

Here is how to use a command button to display a message box. First, you have to create a command button by selecting it from the control toolbox and placing it on the spreadsheet. (Detailed instructions are provided in the "Using the Command Button" section. Next, give the button a name to make it easy to identify it in the code. One approach is to use the word command or an abbreviation like cmd followed by what the button does, i.e. cmdMessageBox. Next, set the caption to tell the user what this button does, for instance MESSAGE BOX. The caption may have spaces between words. Now, double click on the button to open where the code is saved. Initially it will only have a Private Sub ... line and an End Sub line. Your code goes in between. Code is not allowed outside the Sub or subroutine in this case. Other cases do exist, but for now keep all code as shown. Declarations are entered in a different part of the code form.

The text in the message box is simply entered within quotation marks as shown in the following code example.

```
Private Sub cmdMessageBox_Click()

    MsgBox ("This is a Message Box")

End Sub
```

Clicking on OK closes the message box.

There is another way to use the message box that allows a Yes/No response from the user:

```
iReply = MsgBox(Prompt:="Does route
continue?", _
        Buttons:=vbYesNo, Title:="Continue
Route")
If iReply = vbYes Then
  'Do some stuff
End If
If iReply = vbNo Then
  'Do some different stuff
End if
```

iReply is the variable we generally use to store the user's input. Any string variable is allowed. We use the MsgBox command for this. The message-box structure can be as simple as MsgBox ("Hello"), or we can add the arguments above to give the message box a new title and a couple of user-input buttons.

A related command is the *Input Box.*

$$Signal\_Out = InputBox(Prompt:="Path/Source",$$

$$-$$

$$Title:="Fly\ In\ Info",\ Default:="")$$

This command allows you to input a string of data. As indicated in the command, you can provide a prompt and a default response. In the example above, we have elected to provide no default response.

Error Handling

Many things can conspire to cause VBA code to command Excel to do something it does not like, which usually ends in the display of some nondescript error code and a crashed program. : We can approach this in one of two ways: either intercept the error and shepherd the program off to somewhere else, or allow the error to occur and let VBA's debug tools help us find and fix the problem.

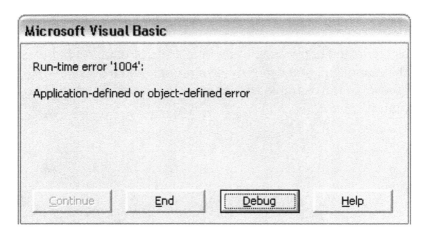

This is the GUI you get when an error has occurred. Not much hint as to what went wrong.

But if you hit *Debug* you are taken to the line of code that had the error.

Here we have a one-line function, and *Debug* has highlighted our one-line program with an error.

```
Sub test()
    ActiveCell.Offset(0, -280).Select
End Sub
```

In this function we asked Excel to move way off the left edge of the sheet.

Let's add a line that tells VBA to go to a spot in the program if an error occurs and display a message.

Sub test( )
   On Error GoTo You_Did_Something_Wrong
   ActiveCell.Offset(0, -280).Select
   Exit Sub
You_Did_Something_Wrong:
   MsgBox ("Oops....Somethings not right")
End Sub

The added code causes the GUI below to be shown when the mistake is encountered.

A couple of new things have been introduced here, the first of which is the *On Error* command. This command must be followed by a *GoTo* statement and a label. Labels are old BASIC constructs that can jump to commands in a function that are run when an error is incurred. Here we can see that the label is aptly named You_Did_Something_Wrong. A label is identified by a colon at the end. VBA will not let you indent a label statement, so it does not allow the usual formatting we follow when writing structured code.

Below the label we added the message-box command that displays the GUI shown here. Also notice the *Exit Sub* command that causes the function to end if everything went right.

Troubleshooting Problems with Code

We just saw how errors can be pointed out. One way to discern if a line of code is causing errors is to add an apostrophe to the beginning of a line of code. VBA interprets that whole line to be

68

a comment for human consumption and ignores it when executing. So we can go to the function that is causing the grief and "comment out" any On Error comments ('On Error). This will cause the VBA debugger to go to the offending line of code when you choose the *Debug* option on the first GUI in the previous section.

We can also add markers to our code that can be used to check its execution at any given point. By selecting View -> Immediate Window in the VBA Project GUI, or simply pressing Ctrl+G, we can open an additional window as seen below.

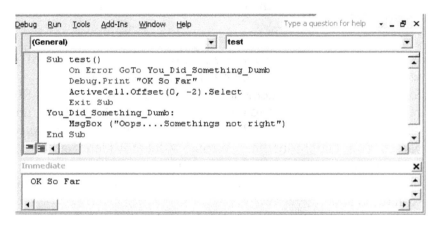

Whenever the code encounters a *Debug.Print* command, it displays the string surrounded by quotes in the window. A drawback to this command is that there is no automatic way to clear the contents in the *Immediate* window. You must do that manually.

The easiest way to start testing new code is by using the F8 key to step through new code. Each time you press the F8 key you execute a single line of code and then step to the next line. This way you will immediately see when you get to a line of code that is causing problems.

As you step through the code, you can hover the cursor above variables to see their current values. This allows you to see how the code is processing various commands.

Another common way to troubleshoot code is to enter breakpoints in the code to cause the code to stop immediately before the line of code with the breakpoint. You can set or reset a breakpoint by selecting a line of code and pressing F9.. By selecting Debug -> Clear All Breakpoints or Ctrl+Shift+F9, you can clear all breakpoints at once.

Below is a simple function that goes down a column 10 rows while filling in each cell it encounters with the line number. The results can be seen at the lower right. Here we have opened the Local window via Views -> Local Window. This window shows us the values of the variable defined in this function. We have also set a breakpoint at the end of each iteration through the *For/Next* loop.

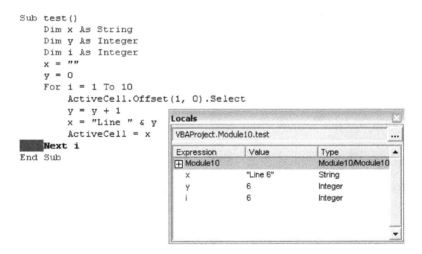

```
Sub test()
    Dim x As String
    Dim y As Integer
    Dim i As Integer
    x = ""
    y = 0
    For i = 1 To 10
        ActiveCell.Offset(1, 0).Select
        y = y + 1
        x = "Line " & y
        ActiveCell = x
    Next i
End Sub
```

Locals
VBAProject.Module10.test

Expression	Value	Type
⊞ Module10		Module10/Module10
x	"Line 6"	String
y	6	Integer
i	6	Integer

Line 1
Line 2
Line 3
Line 4
Line 5
Line 6

Here you can see that we are at the sixth iteration through the loop (i = 6).

```
Sub test()
    Dim x As String
    Dim y As Integer
    Dim i As Integer
    x = ""
    y = 0
    For i = 1 To 10
        ActiveCell.Offset(1, 0).Select
        y = y + 1
        x = "Line " & y
        ActiveCell = x
    Next i
    Debug.Assert (y > 12)
End Sub
```

We can also force the execution of code to stop if a condition is not met.

Here we added the command *Debug.Assert* and a condition in parentheses.

At the end of the program y was not greater than 12, so execution of the code stopped.

Another great debugging tool is the *Watch* command. This is initiated by
View - > Watch Window. We can then define what we want to watch by

Debug -> Add Watch.

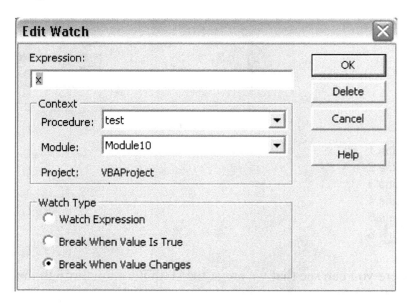

From the Debug menu selection we can Add a Watch or Edit an existing Watch.

We select the variable we want to watch and then select one of three Watch types.

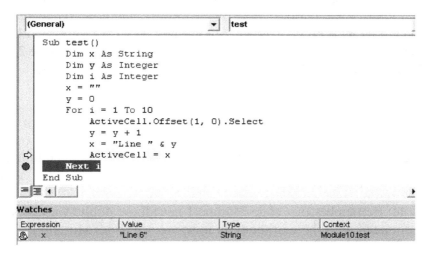

Because we selected *Break When Value Changes*, the code stops execution whenever the value of the watched variable changes. Here we see that execution has stopped before the next line of code because the value of x has changed.

40 Nifty Things You Can Do With Excel

Managing The Workbook (Module 2)

In this first section we'll see how we can manipulate, control, and interrogate worksheets in our workbook and how to manage the whole workbook. To help you use and become familiar with these routines, the workbook has a worksheet named **Module 2 Examples(MOD 2 EX)** that lists all the functions associated with the Managing the Workbook section.

All the routines associated with this section are in Module 2 of the VBA add-in file that comes with this book. From here on out each new section will have its own worksheet and code module associated with it.

Note: Remember that code Module 1 has all the public variables associated with the workbook in it, so we start with Module 2.

Now we start with the routines that will put Excel under your command.

On the MOD 2 EX worksheet you will find that column A has a number of lists. The bold title of each list has a comment in its cell that tells you how to activate the VBA code to act upon that list.

In the case of the **GENERATE WORKSHEETS** list, which calls Generate_Necessary_Worksheets when *ALT + g* are pressed, any spreadsheets not currently in existence that are in the list are generated.

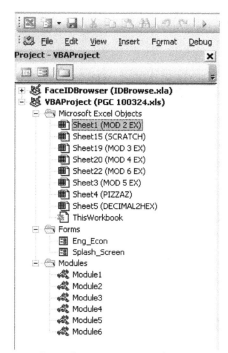

Here you can see the worksheet objects that are originally part of the associated software from the VBA project editor. The sheet numbers correspond to the order in which sheets have been created. Ignore those. The names in parantheses are the names referred to in this book. The sheets listed here are the sheets the come originally with the software.

When you run Generate_Necessary_Workshe ets any entries found in the **GENERATE WORKSHEETS** list that are not found are generated.

We will see shortly how to hide and unhide sheets in the workbook.

REMINDER: You can always manually hide or unhide sheets via Format -> Sheet -> Hide/Unhide

So the procedure below looks at the list below **GENERATE WORKSHEETS** and generates spreadsheets with the names in the list if they don't already exist.

Automatically Create New Worksheets

```
Sub Generate_Necessary_Worksheets()
    'Automatically create a new worksheet**************
    On Error Resume Next
    Dim temp As String
    Count = 0
    Call List_WorkSheets
    Sheets("MOD 2 EX").Visible = True
```

74

```
Sheets("MOD 2 EX").Select
Range("A1").Select
Do
        If ActiveCell = "GENERATE WORKSHEETS" Then
                ActiveCell.Offset(1, 0).Select
                Exit Do
        Else:
                ActiveCell.Offset(1, 0).Select
                Count = Count + 1
                If Count > 1000 Then
                    Range("A1").Select
                    MsgBox ("GENERATE WORKSHEETS not
                    found")
                    Exit Sub
                End If
        End If
    Loop
'Now collect sheet name and color index number, find next
open row
'in SCRATCH worksheet and enter new sheet if it does not
already exist
'Outer Do loop
    Do
        If ActiveCell = "" Then
                Exit Do
        End If
        Sheet_Name = ActiveCell
        Sheet_Name = UCase(ActiveCell)
        ActiveCell.Offset(0, 1).Select
        Tab_Color = ActiveCell
        ActiveCell.Offset(1, -1).Select
        Sheets("SCRATCH").Select
        Range("A1").Select
        'Inner Do loop
            Do
                If ActiveCell = Sheet_Name Then
                    Exit Do
                Else:
                    ActiveCell.Offset(1, 0).Select
                End If
```

75

```
            If ActiveCell = "" Then
              'End of SCRATCH sheet list - sheet must not
              exist - so add
                Sheets.Add
                temp =
Application.Parent.ActiveSheet.Name
                Sheets(temp).Select
                Sheets(temp).Move
Before:=Sheets("SCRATCH")

                ActiveWorkbook.Sheets(temp).Tab.ColorIndex = _
                Tab_Color
                Sheets(temp).Name = Sheet_Name
                Exit Do
            End If
          Loop
          Call List_WorkSheets
          Sheets("MOD 2 EX").Select
      Loop
      Sheets("MOD 2 EX").Select
End Sub
```

Here's our first piece of real code. This procedure finds a list of
worksheets and their assigned ColorIndex number on the MOD 2
EX worksheet. It checks to see if a particular worksheet exists,
and if not, it creates it and assigns it a tab color based on the
ColorIndex number.

This starts off by assigning a local variable called temp and
setting a public variable called Count to 0. It then updates the
worksheet list, makes sure the MOD 2 EX worksheet is open and
selects it, and goes to cell A1.

This procedure then goes down column A until it finds a cell
called GENERATE WORKSHEETS, exits the first *Do* loop, and
moves on to the next steps. If it never finds the required cell
(after 1,000 rows) it generates a "GENERATE WORKSHEETS
not found" message and then exits the entire subroutine.

Now each entry on the MOD 2 EX list is checked via the outer *Do* loop and compared with the list on the "SCRATCH" worksheet to see if there is an entry indicating that the sheet already exists. If the end of the list on the SCRATCH sheet is reached, then the sheet must not yet exist and it is added.

By adding to the list on the MOD 2 EX sheet, you can automatically add sheets to the workbook.

List Worksheets

```
Sub List_WorkSheets()
    Sheets("SCRATCH").Visible = True
    Sheets("SCRATCH").Select
    Range("A1").Select
    Range("A1:D100").Select
    Selection.ClearContents
    For Each ws In Worksheets
        Color = "*"
        ActiveCell = ws.Name
        Tab_Color = ws.Tab.ColorIndex
        Call Color_Number_to_Name
        ActiveCell.Offset(0, 3).Select
        ActiveCell = Color
        ActiveCell.Offset(1, -3).Select
    Next ws
    Range("A1").Select
End Sub

Sub Color_Number_to_Name()
    Select Case Tab_Color
        Case Is = 1
            Color = "BLACK"
        Case Is = 2
            Color = "WHITE"
        Case Is = 3
            Color = "RED"
        Case Is = 4
            Color = "GREEN"
```

```
           Case Is = 5
                Color = "BLUE"
           Case Is = 6
                Color = "YELLOW"
           Case Is = 7
                Color = "VIOLET"
           Case Is = 8
                Color = "CYAN"
           Case Is = 15
                Color = "GRAY"
      End Select
End Sub
```

This procedure calls a second procedure called
Color_Number_to_Name.

The main procedure goes through all the existing sheets in our
workbook and lists them in columns A and D on the SCRATCH
worksheet.

It does this by unhiding the SCRATCH worksheet, if it is hidden
(otherwise the Visible = True statement has no effect) and then
selecting that sheet. The code then goes to cell A1 and clears
everything in columns A and D and rows 1 through100.

The *For/Next* statement now tells Excel to list each worksheet,
one at a time. The worksheets, and their corresponding colors?,
are loaded into objects called ws.Name and ws.Tab.ColorIndex
(and then transferred to Tab_Color). Each worksheet name is
loaded into the next cell down on the SCRATCH worksheet,
starting at cell A1.

The *Select Case* in the second procedure assigns a color name to
the *Color.Index* number. After the *End Select* statement the code
moves over three columns to the D column and loads color into
the *ActiveCell*.

By changing the Color = "Name" in the Select statements you
can assign any name to a worksheet tab color.

The second list on the MOD 2 EX spreadsheet is associated with the procedure below. It alternately unhides and hides sheets based on the list below **HIDE/UNHIDE WORKSHEETS**. It looks for matches between the letters in the list and the corresponding first letters in a spreadsheet. If it finds a match it hides the spreadsheet if visible and unhides it if it is currently hidden.

Automatically Hide and Unhide Worksheets

```
Sub Hide_UnHide_Sheets()
    'Automatic Hide and Unhide Worksheets******
        On Error Resume Next
            Word_Length = 0
        Sheet_Name = ""
        Eng_Econ_Display = False
        Sheets("SCRATCH").Visible = True
        Sheets("MOD 2 EX").Visible = True
        Sheets("MOD 2 EX").Select
        Range("A1").Select
        Do
                If ActiveCell = "HIDE/UNHIDE WORKSHEETS"
Then
                        ActiveCell.Offset(1, 0).Select
                        Last_Cell =
                        ActiveWindow.RangeSelection.Address
                        Exit Do
                Else:
                        ActiveCell.Offset(1, 0).Select
                        Count = Count + 1
                        If Count > 1000 Then
                            Range("A1").Select
                            MsgBox ("HIDE/UNHIDE WORKSHEETS
                            not found")
                            Exit Sub
                        End If
                End If
        Loop
        'Sheet Color Selected
        Do
```

```
If Left(ActiveCell, 1) = "#" Then
    Tab_Color = Right(ActiveCell, Len(ActiveCell)
    - 1)
    Call Color_Number_to_Name
    Sheets("SCRATCH").Visible = True
    Sheets("SCRATCH").Select
    Range("D1").Select
        'Find color matches between values
        found in 'Color_Number_to_Name
        'and values in column D of the SCRATCH
        worksheet
        Do
    If ActiveCell = Color Then
            ActiveCell.Offset(0, -3).Select
            Sheet_Name = ActiveCell
                If
            Sheets(Sheet_Name).Visible =
            True Then
            Sheets(Sheet_Name).Visible =
            False
            Else:
            Sheets(Sheet_Name).Visible =
            True
            End If
            ActiveCell.Offset(0, 3).Select
        End If
        If ActiveCell = "" Then
                Exit Do
        End If
        ActiveCell.Offset(1, 0).Select
    Loop
End If
Sheets("MOD 2 EX").Visible = True
Sheets("MOD 2 EX").Select
ActiveCell.Offset(1, 0).Select
If ActiveCell = "" Then
    Exit Do
End If
Loop
Sheets("MOD 2 EX").Visible = True
```

```
Sheets("MOD 2 EX").Select
Range(Last_Cell).Select
 'Partial or complete sheet name selected
Do
        Word_Length = Len(ActiveCell)
        Sheet_Name = UCase(ActiveCell)
        Sheets("SCRATCH").Visible = True
        Sheets("SCRATCH").Select
        Range("A1").Select
        Do
                Scratch_Name = ActiveCell
                If Left(Scratch_Name, Word_Length) =
                Sheet_Name Then
                    If Sheets(Scratch_Name).Visible = True The
                        Sheets(Scratch_Name).Visible = False
                    Else:
                        Sheets(Scratch_Name).Visible = True
                    End If
                End If
                If ActiveCell = "" Then
                    Exit Do
                End If
                ActiveCell.Offset(1, 0).Select
        Loop
        Sheets("MOD 2 EX").Visible = True
        Sheets("MOD 2 EX").Select
        ActiveCell.Offset(1, 0).Select
        If ActiveCell = "" Then
                Exit Do
        End If
Loop
Eng_Econ_Display = True
End Sub
```

We start this routine by setting *Eng_Econ_Display = False*. We also make visible a couple of worksheets and select "MOD 2 EX." This is the Module 2 Examples worksheet, upon which we have a list of worksheets we want to alternately hide or unhide.

We then go to the top of the worksheet and go down the A column looking for a cell with the contents "HIDE/UNHIDE WORKSHEETS" via the first *Do* loop. When we find that cell we move down one additional cell and then exit the loop. At this point we remember that cell's location for future use via *Last_Cell = ActiveWindow.RangeSelection.Address*.

If after 1,000 cells we don't find a cell with "HIDE/UNHIDE WORKSHEETS," we then display the message "HIDE/UNHIDE WORKSHEETS not found" and exit the entire subroutine.

Moving on to the second *Do* loop under the 'Sheet Color Selected comment, we start down the list of worksheets to hide or unhide looking for any that start with a number sign, indicating that these entries represent a color and not a sheet name. The variable *Tab_Color* contains the color value, which is used by calling the routine Color_Number_to_Name (defined earlier) to link the number value to an actual Excel color.

Within the second *Do* loop is another nested *Do* loop. The outer *Do* loop checks the hide/unhide list on the MOD 2 EX worksheet, while the inner *Do* loop is used to check worksheet colors on the SCRATCH worksheet.

At this point the SCRATCH worksheet is selected, and the worksheet colors starting at cell D1 are each checked to see if any of the color values match the value found by the Color_Number_to_Name routine. If a match is found, then the cell three places to the left (column A) is accessed to capture the value Sheet_Name. This value is then used to make that sheet visible if it is currently hidden, and invisible if it is currently visible.

When a blank cell is found in the worksheet color list on the SCRATCH sheet, then the nested *Do* loop within the second *Do* loop is exited. You'll notice that the MOD 2 EX worksheet is commanded to unhide, just in case it was accidentally closed.

The outer Do loop continues down the Hide/Unhide list on the MOD 2 EX worksheet until it encounters a blank cell. At this point, we are done looking for worksheet tab colors and move on to searching for worksheet tab text. So we go back to the cell pointed at in *Last_Cell*. We now start down the Hide/Unhide list again.

Now we are looking for any partial matches in the Hide/Unhide list and the worksheet list in column A of the SCRATCH worksheet. The outer *Do* loop of this next section does that on the list on the MOD 2 EX worksheet by capturing the value of a cell in the list via the *Sheet_Name* variable (which is also converted to uppercase for search on the SCRATCH list because all our worksheets are in uppercase). The length of the string that corresponds to the *Sheet_Name* value is also captured via *Word_Length*.

The inner *Do* loop goes down column A on the SCRATCH worksheet looking for partial matches via the *If/Then Left(Scratch_Name, Word_Length) = Sheet_Name* statement. Again, any matches result in the opposite of a sheet's current hide/unhide status.

This routine ends with *Eng_Econ_Display = True*, which we will see the significance of in the next section.

There are a number of other options on the MOD 2 EX worksheet. We will look at a number of these latest. By holding the cursor over the marked cells will indicate the command to activate the associated functions.

Actions When the Worksheet is Opened/Closed

Want something to happen when a worksheet sheet is selected?
Add a subroutine on that particular sheet with the name
Worksheet_Activate.

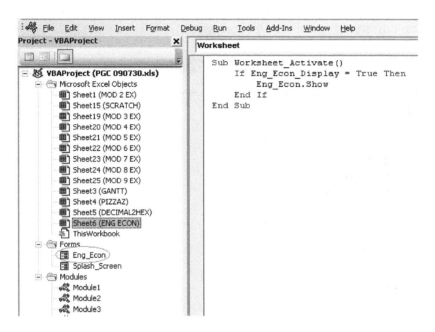

Here we've added a short routine to display the *Eng_Econ* form
(circled) whenever the ENG ECON worksheet is selected, and
the Boolean statement *Eng_Econ_Display* equals true.
Remember in the last section we set the *Eng_Econ* statement to
False at the beginning of the routine and reset it to True at the
end? This was done because when a form is opened it stops all
further execution of your program (outside of actions the form
requires) until the form is closed. We didn't want that distraction,
so we disabled the form from showing during
Hide_UnHide_Sheets() runtime.

Make Things Happen at Startup

You can customize what Excel does at start-up and shutdown. In the graphic below, there is an object called *ThisWorkbook*. If you create a subroutine called *Workbook_Open*, all the commands located within it will be run at Excel start-up. Here we only have one command, a call to *Open_App*.

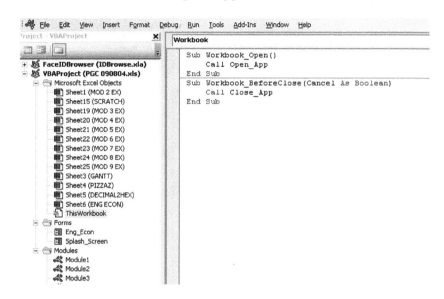

Sub Open_App( )
    Closing_in_Progress = False
    Call create_toolbars
    Call Hide_Command_Bars
    Call Hide_Sheets
    Splash_Screen.Show
    Application.CommandBars("Project").Visible = True
End Sub

In the routine *Open_App*, we set a Boolean value to false (we will cover this shortly) and then call or run several other routines. The first one creates the toolbars that we will use throughout this workbook. We will cover their creation in the next section. The Hide_Command_Bars routine hides those created toolbars until they are needed. But the very last line displays the Project toolbar because that toolbar allows us to open quickly any part of the workbook.

We then hide all the unnecessary workbooks so as not to clutter the display bar below with unnecessary worksheet tabs.

Next we call one of our forms –*Splash_Screen*, which is an opening welcome screen. The constructed form and its main property window (called up by right clicking on any blank area in the form) are shown below.

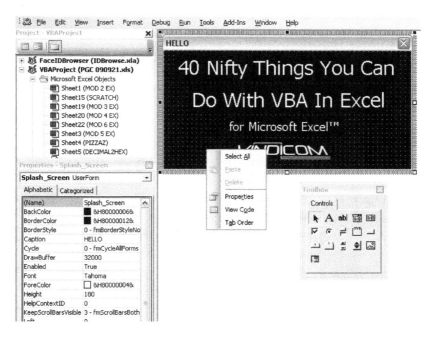

Also, by right clicking on any blank area on the form, you can view the code associated with the form.

A private sub UserForm_Activate is associated with the code for this form. Any subroutine with this name on the user form code module will run when the form is opened. The form was opened via the *Splash_Screen.Show* command called in the *Workbook_Open* routine.

The two commands in the *UserForm_Activate* routine are to halt the running of the program for approximately three seconds and then unload or close the form.

The graphic above shows that the *ThisWorkbook* object also has a *Workbook_BeforeClose* routine, which calls a *Close_App* routine that can be found in Module 2. The routine deletes the toolbars that were created when the program opened. The routine is listed below.

Sub Close_App()
    On Error Resume Next
    Application.StatusBar = False
    Closing_in_Progress = True
    Call *Unhide_Command_Bars*
    Call *Delete_Command_Bars*
    ActiveWorkbook.Save
    Application.Quit
End Sub

The above routine is called by the *Workbook_BeforeClose* function on the *ThisWorkbook* object whenever the program is closed. The On Error Resume Next command is fairly straightforward: Essentially, it tells Excel if an error is encountered, ignore it and move on. Errors might be encountered in the *Delete_Command_Bars* function if toolbars slated to be deleted have already been deleted somehow. The Boolean variable *Closing_in_Progress* is not used anywhere. We currently include two instances of it: *Closing_in_Progress = False* during *Workbook_Open* and the second instance as seen above.

We will cover the Unhide_Command_Bars and Delete_Command_Bars in the "Restoring toolbars when closing" section. Finally, the last two commands save the workbook before closing it.

Create Workbook Toolbars

The following toolbars are created by the *Call create_toolbars* command in the *Workbook_Open* function during startup.

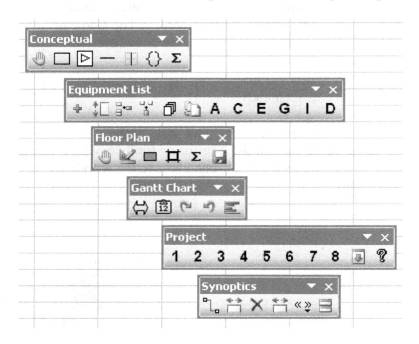

The function to create toolbars is by far the longest to this point. But much of it is repetitious. Once you understand how to create one toolbar, the others follow the same procedure.

We start with:
Application.CommandBars.Add(Name:="Name_of_Toolbar").Visible = True

We then add controls to the toolbar:
Set Control_Name =
Application.CommandBars("Name_of_Toolbar").Controls.Add _
    (Type:=msoControlButton)
Next we add attributes to the control:
With Control_Name
    .FaceId = 51

.OnAction = "Format_Conceptual"
.Caption = "Format Conceptual"
End With

FaceId is the icon to be displayed for the control. (More on this later.)
OnAction is the routine to called or run when the control is selected.
Caption is the text to be displayed when the cursor is held over the icon.

Now we will list the code for creating our toolbars.

```
Sub create_toolbars()
      On Error Resume Next
      Dim x As Long
      Dim y As Long
      '***********Project
Toolbar***********************
      Application.CommandBars.Add(Name:="Project").Visible
      = True
      x = GetSystemMetrics32(SM_CXScreen)
      y = GetSystemMetrics32(SM_CYScreen)
      With Project
            .StartUpPosition = 0
            .Top = (y - .Height) * 0.9
            .Left = (x - .Width) * 0.9
            .Show
      End With
      Set Open_1 =
Application.CommandBars("Project").Controls.Add _
            (Type:=msoControlButton)
      With Open_1
            .FaceId = 71
            .OnAction = ""
                  .Caption = "Module 1" & Chr(10) & "Contains
                  all the workbooks public variables"
      End With
      Set Open_2 =
Application.CommandBars("Project").Controls.Add _
```

```
        (Type:=msoControlButton)
    With Open_2
        .FaceId = 72
        .OnAction = "Mod_2"
        .Caption = "Module 2" & Chr(10) & "Managing the
Workbook"
    End With
    Set Open_3 =
Application.CommandBars("Project").Controls.Add _
        (Type:=msoControlButton)
    With Open_3
        .FaceId = 73
        .OnAction = "Mod_3"
        .Caption = "Module 3" & Chr(10) & "Drawing"
    End With
    Set Open_4 =
Application.CommandBars("Project").Controls.Add _
        (Type:=msoControlButton)
    With Open_4
        .FaceId = 74
        .OnAction = "Mod_4"
        .Caption = "Module 4" & Chr(10) & "Finance"
    End With
    Set Open_5 =
Application.CommandBars("Project").Controls.Add _
        (Type:=msoControlButton)
    With Open_5
        .FaceId = 75
        .OnAction = "Mod_5"
        .Caption = "Module 5" & Chr(10) & "Project
Planning"
    End With
    Set Open_6 =
Application.CommandBars("Project").Controls.Add _
        (Type:=msoControlButton)
    With Open_6
        .FaceId = 76
        .OnAction = "Mod_6"
        .Caption = "Module 6" & Chr(10) & "Generate a
        Floor Plan"
```

```
End With
Set Open_7 =
Application.CommandBars("Project").Controls.Add _
      (Type:=msoControlButton)
With Open_7
      .FaceId = 77
      .OnAction = "Mod_7"
      .Caption = "Module 7" & Chr(10) & "Managing
Inventories"
End With
Set Open_8 =
Application.CommandBars("Project").Controls.Add _
      (Type:=msoControlButton)
With Open_8
      .FaceId = 78
      .OnAction = "Mod_8"
      .Caption = "Module 8" & Chr(10) & "Shipping"
End With
Set Open_9 =
Application.CommandBars("Project").Controls.Add _
      (Type:=msoControlButton)
With Open_9
      .FaceId = 79
      .OnAction = "Pizzazz"
      .Caption = "Pizzazz" & Chr(10) & "Sound and
Video"
End With
      Set Close_Project_Worksheets =
            Application.CommandBars("Project").Controls.A
            dd _
            (Type:=msoControlButton)
With Close_Project_Worksheets
      .FaceId = 372
      .OnAction = "Hide_Sheets"
      .Caption = "Hide all worksheets except MOD 2 EX
      and SCRATCH"
End With
```

************Create Drawing Toolbar************

```
Application.CommandBars.Add(Name:="Project
Drawing").Visible = True
    Set Make_Drawing_Block =
        Application.CommandBars("Project
        Drawing").Controls.Add _
    (Type:=msoControlButton)
With Make_Drawing_Block
    .FaceId = 131
    .OnAction = "Make_a_Box"
    .Caption = "Create a Box"
End With
    Set Make_Drawing_Triangle =
        Application.CommandBars("Project
        Drawing").Controls.Add _
    (Type:=msoControlButton)
With Make_Drawing_Triangle
    .FaceId = 2924
    .OnAction = "Make_a_Triangle"
    .Caption = "Create a Triangle"
End With
    Set Create_Drawing_Line =
        Application.CommandBars("Project
        Drawing").Controls.Add _
    (Type:=msoControlButton)
With Create_Drawing_Line
    .FaceId = 613
    .OnAction = "Create_Horizontal_Line"
    .Caption = "Create a Horizontal Line"
End With
    Set Create_Vertical_V_Line =
        Application.CommandBars("Project
        Drawing").Controls.Add _
    (Type:=msoControlButton)
With Create_Vertical_V_Line
    .FaceId = 1841
    .OnAction = "Create_a_Vertical_Line"
    .Caption = "Create a Vertical Line"
End With
```

```
    Set Create_Complex_Line =
        Application.CommandBars("Project
        Drawing").Controls.Add _
        (Type:=msoControlButton)
With Create_Complex_Line
    .FaceId = 732
    .OnAction = "Create_a_Complete_Line"
    .Caption = "Create a Complex Line" & Chr(10) & "Hold
        CTRL and select 3 points" & Chr(10) & _
            "Points 1,2,3 must be left to right in order"
End With
    Set Create_Drawing_Special_Character =
        Application.CommandBars("Project
        Drawing").Controls.Add _
        (Type:=msoControlButton)
With Create_Drawing_Special_Character
    .FaceId = 346
    .OnAction = "Create_Special_Character"
    .Caption = "Insert a Special Character"
End With
    Set Create_Drawing_Rack =
        Application.CommandBars("Project
        Drawing").Controls.Add _
        (Type:=msoControlButton)
With Create_Drawing_Rack
    .FaceId = 438
    .OnAction = "Rack_Elevation"
    .Caption = "Create Equipment Racks"
End With

    ***********Equipment List Toolbar***********
Application.CommandBars.Add(Name:="Equipment
List").Visible = True
    Set Add_to_Eq_List =
        Application.CommandBars("Equipment
        List").Controls.Add _
        (Type:=msoControlButton)
With Add_to_Eq_List
    .FaceId = 137
    .OnAction = "Select_From_Eq_Library"
```

94

```
        .Caption = "Add equipment to list"
End With
  Set Expand_the_Equipment_List =
         Application.CommandBars("Equipment
         List").Controls.Add _
         (Type:=msoControlButton)
With Expand_the_Equipment_List
    .FaceId = 541
    .OnAction = "Expand_Eq_List"
    .Caption = "Explode the equipment list"
End With
  Set Stuff_Equipment_In_Racks =
         Application.CommandBars("Equipment
         List").Controls.Add _
         (Type:=msoControlButton)
With Stuff_Equipment_In_Racks
    .FaceId = 295
    .OnAction = "Stuff_Racks"
    .Caption = "Stuff equipment into racks"
End With
  Set Stuff_Cards_In_Frames =
         Application.CommandBars("Equipment
         List").Controls.Add _
         (Type:=msoControlButton)
With Stuff_Cards_In_Frames
    .FaceId = 297
    .OnAction = "Stuff_Frames"
    .Caption = "Stuff cards into frames"
End With
  Set Build_Drawing_Set =
         Application.CommandBars("Equipment
         List").Controls.Add _
         (Type:=msoControlButton)
With Build_Drawing_Set
    .FaceId = 53
    .OnAction = "Generate_Necessary_Worksheets"
    .Caption = "Generate required drawings"
End With
```

```
    Set Load_Drawings =
        Application.CommandBars("Equipment
        List").Controls.Add _
          (Type:=msoControlButton)
    With Load_Drawings
        .FaceId = 159
        .OnAction = "Load_into_Food_Chain"
        .Caption = "Load equipment from list into drawings"
    End With
      Set Sort_A = Application.CommandBars("Equipment
            List").Controls.Add _
        (Type:=msoControlButton)
    With Sort_A
        .FaceId = 80
        .OnAction = "Sort_Eq_List_by_Item"
        .Caption = "Sort equipment list by column A"
    End With
      Set Sort_C = Application.CommandBars("Equipment
            List").Controls.Add _
        (Type:=msoControlButton)
    With Sort_C
        .FaceId = 82
        .OnAction = "Sort_Eq_List_by_Mfgr"
        .Caption = "Sort equipment list by column C"
    End With
    Set Sort_E = Application.CommandBars("Equipment
List").Controls.Add _
        (Type:=msoControlButton)
    With Sort_E
        .FaceId = 84
        .OnAction = "Sort_Eq_List_by_System"
        .Caption = "Sort equipment list by column E"
    End With
    Set Sort_G = Application.CommandBars("Equipment
List").Controls.Add _
        (Type:=msoControlButton)
    With Sort_G
        .FaceId = 86
        .OnAction = "Sort_Eq_List_by_DRW_and_FC"
        .Caption = "Sort equipment list by column G"
```

```vba
    End With
    Set Sort_I = Application.CommandBars("Equipment
List").Controls.Add _
        (Type:=msoControlButton)
    With Sort_I
        .FaceId = 88
        .OnAction = "Sort_Eq_List_by_Location"
        .Caption = "Sort equipment list by column I"
    End With
    Set Sort_D = Application.CommandBars("Equipment
List").Controls.Add _
        (Type:=msoControlButton)
    With Sort_D
        .FaceId = 83
        .OnAction = "Sort_Eq_List_by_Description"
        .Caption = "Sort equipment list by column D"
    End With

        ***********Floor Plan Toolbar***********
    Application.CommandBars.Add(Name:="Floor
    Plan").Visible = True
    Set New_Flr_Pln = Application.CommandBars("Floor
    Plan").Controls.Add _
        (Type:=msoControlButton)
    With New_Flr_Pln
        .FaceId = 51
        .OnAction = "Make_Floor_?Plan_Ready"
        .Caption = "Create New Floor Plan"
    End With
    Set Outline_Facility = Application.CommandBars("Floor
    Plan").Controls.Add _
        (Type:=msoControlButton)
    With Outline_Facility
        .FaceId = 1081
        .OnAction = "Make_Facility"
        .Caption = "Create Facility Outline" & Chr(10) &
    "Select 3 points first"
    End With
    Set Outline_Room = Application.CommandBars("Floor
    Plan").Controls.Add _
```

(Type:=msoControlButton)
With Outline_Room
    .FaceId = 412
    .OnAction = "Make_Room"
    .Caption = "Create Room Outline" & Chr(10) & _
        "Highlight Room area, then Ctrl and Select
        Room color"
End With
Set Row_of_Racks = Application.CommandBars("Floor
Plan").Controls.Add _
    (Type:=msoControlButton)
With Row_of_Racks
    .FaceId = 388
    .OnAction = "Make_Racks"
    .Caption = "Make a row of racks" & Chr(10) & _
        "Highlight Rack Row Area (2 Wide by # of
        Racks (2 wide each))"
End With
Set Tally_the_Racks = Application.CommandBars("Floor
Plan").Controls.Add _
    (Type:=msoControlButton)
With Tally_the_Racks
    .FaceId = 226
    .OnAction = "Tally_Racks"
    .Caption = "Tally Racks" & Chr(10) & _
        "Select 2 points covering area to be checked" &
        Chr(10) & _
        "WARNING - This will wipe out current rack
        elevations"
End With
  Set Save_Copy_Flr_Pln =
        Application.CommandBars("Floor
        Plan").Controls.Add _
    (Type:=msoControlButton)
With Save_Copy_Flr_Pln
    .FaceId = 3
    .OnAction = "Save_Floor_Plan"
    .Caption = "Create a copy of this Floor Plan"
End With

************_Gantt Chart Toolbar_************

```
Application.CommandBars.Add(Name:="Gantt
Chart").Visible = True
    Set Set_Start_Stop_Dates =
            Application.CommandBars("Gantt
            Chart").Controls.Add _
        (Type:=msoControlButton)
    With Set_Start_Stop_Dates
        .FaceId = 1146
        .OnAction = "Select_Start_End_Dates"
        .Caption = "Select project start and end dates"
    End With
    Set List_Project_Tasks =
            Application.CommandBars("Gantt
            Chart").Controls.Add _
        (Type:=msoControlButton)
    With List_Project_Tasks
        .FaceId = 370
        .OnAction = "List_Tasks"
        .Caption = "List project tasks"
    End With
    Set Save_Project_Dates =
            Application.CommandBars("Gantt
            Chart").Controls.Add _
        (Type:=msoControlButton)
    With Save_Project_Dates
        .FaceId = 129
        .OnAction = "Save_Dates"
        .Caption = "Save project dates"
    End With
    Set Recall_Project_Dates =
            Application.CommandBars("Gantt
            Chart").Controls.Add _
        (Type:=msoControlButton)
    With Recall_Project_Dates
        .FaceId = 128
        .OnAction = "Recall_Previous_Dates"
        .Caption = "Recall project dates"
    End With
```

```
Set Project_Timelines =
        Application.CommandBars("Gantt
        Chart").Controls.Add
        _(Type:=msoControlButton)
With Project_Timelines
    .FaceId = 419
    .OnAction = "Create_Time?lines"
    .Caption = "Create project timelines"
End With


***********Synoptic Toolbar*************
Application.CommandBars.Add(Name:="Synoptics").Visib
le = True
Set Create_Route =
Application.CommandBars("Synoptics").Controls.Add _
        (Type:=msoControlButton)
With Create_Route
    .FaceId = 1043
    .OnAction = "Make_Route"
    .Caption = "Create a new route"
End With
  Set Create_Flys =
        Application.CommandBars("Synoptics").Controls
        .Add _
        (Type:=msoControlButton)
With Create_Flys
    .FaceId = 542
    .OnAction = "Make_FlyOff"
    .Caption = "Create a new fly on or off"
End With
Set Erase_Route =
Application.CommandBars("Synoptics").Controls.Add _
        (Type:=msoControlButton)
With Erase_Route
    .FaceId = 358
    .OnAction = "EraseRoute"
    .Caption = "Erase a route"
End With
Set Create_Flys =
Application.CommandBars("Synoptics").Controls.Add _
```

```
                    (Type:=msoControlButton)
    With Create_Flys
          .FaceId = 542
          .OnAction = "Make_FlyOnOff"
          .Caption = "Create a new fly on or off"
    End With
       Set CompilePatching =
                Application.CommandBars("Synoptics").Controls
                .Add _
          (Type:=msoControlButton)
    With CompilePatching
          .FaceId = 158
          .OnAction = "Compile_Patching"
          .Caption = "Compile Synoptic Patching"
    End With
    Set Check_Flyons_offs =
    Application.CommandBars("Synoptics").Controls.Add _
          (Type:=msoControlButton)
    With Check_Flyons_offs
          .FaceId = 298
          .OnAction = "Check_FlyOnsOffs"
          .Caption = "Check fly ons match fly offs"
    End With
```

********Hide created toolbars except Project********

```
    Application.CommandBars("Conceptual").Visible = False
    Application.CommandBars("Floor Plan").Visible = False
    Application.CommandBars("Equipment List").Visible =
    False
    Application.CommandBars("Gantt Chart").Visible = False
    Application.CommandBars("Synoptics").Visible = False
End Sub
```

To help you determine the FaceID of an icon you want to use, a software consultant named Shyam Pillai maintains a website that has a most useful toolbar add-in called FaceID Browser. This add-in allows you to quickly determine the ID number of an icon you wish to use. It can be found at http://skp.mvps.org/faceid.htm. Once his program is downloaded and unzipped, you can add it by going to Tools -> Add-Ins and browsing to its location, selecting it, and then clicking OK. It will now be available for use.

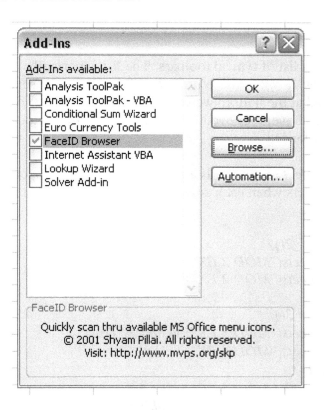

You can now go to View -> Toolbars and select the *FaceID Browser* toolbar to be displayed.

This is what the toolbar looks like. By hovering the cursor over an icon you can see the *FaceID* number for a particular icon. For example, the *FaceID* number for the numeral 3 is 73.

There are literally thousands of FaceIDs spread out over 10,000 ID values. Many FaceID numbers have no currently assigned icon.

Here is a list of typical toolbars. The list is normally what Excel provides, down to the WordArt toolbar. Six of the seven toolbars outlined at the bottom were created by the *Create_Toolbars* routine above; the seventh is the *FaceID Browser* toolbar add-in we just loaded..

The *Project* toolbar calls a number of routines to open the proper worksheets when each control is selected. Below are those routines.

```
Sub Mod_2()
     Sheets("MOD 2 EX").Visible = True
     Sheets("MOD 2 EX").Select
End Sub
Sub Mod_3()
     Sheets("MOD 3 EX").Visible = True
     Sheets("MOD 3 EX").Select
End Sub
Sub Mod_4()
     Sheets("MOD 4 EX").Visible = True
     Sheets("MOD 4 EX").Select
End Sub
Sub Mod_5()
     Sheets("MOD 5 EX").Visible = True
     Sheets("MOD 5 EX").Select
End Sub
Sub Mod_6()
     Sheets("MOD 6 EX").Visible = True
     Sheets("MOD 6 EX").Select
End Sub
Sub Mod_7()
     Sheets("MOD 7 EX").Visible = True
     Sheets("MOD 7 EX").Select
End Sub
Sub Mod_8()
```

```
        Sheets("MOD 8 EX").Visible = True
        Sheets("MOD 8 EX").Select
End Sub
Sub Pizzazz()
        Sheets("PIZZAZZ").Visible = True
        Sheets("PIZZAZZ").Select
End Sub
```

Set Which Toolbars are Displayed

Now that we have created toolbars, we want to be able to hide them and display them automatically without having to manually select or deselect them through the *View* menu. We accomplish this with two functions. The first lists the toolbars open and stores that list in the M column of the SCRATCH worksheet. The function then, via a *For/Next* loop, closes all the toolbars listed. Remember, the list will be comprised of only the open toolbars. If none are open to begin with, then the list will be blank.

```
Sub Hide_Command_Bars()
    Dim CB As CommandBar
    Sheets("SCRATCH").Visible = True
    Sheets("SCRATCH").Select
    Columns("M:M").Select
    Selection.ClearContents
    Range("M1").Select
    For Each CB In CommandBars
        If CB.Type = msoBarTypeNormal Then
            If CB.Visible Then
            CBNum = CB.index
            CB.Visible = False
            ActiveCell = CB.Name
            ActiveCell.Offset(1, 0).Select
        End If
        End If
    Next CB
End Sub
```

The function below simply reads the list of toolbars in column M of the SCRATCH worksheet and makes all in the list visible.

```
Sub Unhide_Command_Bars()
    Dim Name As String
    Sheets("SCRATCH").Visible = True
    Sheets("SCRATCH").Select
    Range("M1").Select
```

```
        Do
                Name = ActiveCell
                On Error Resume Next
                Application.CommandBars(Name).Visible = True
                ActiveCell.Offset(1, 0).Select
                If ActiveCell = "" Then
                        Exit Do
                End If
        Loop
End Sub
```

Restore Toolbar List to Normal when Closing

To eliminate the toolbars from the toolbar list when the workbook is closed, we run the routine below.

```
Sub Delete_Command_Bars()
        On Error Resume Next
        CommandBars("Conceptual").Delete
        CommandBars("Floor Plan").Delete
        CommandBars("Equipment List").Delete
        CommandBars("Gantt Chart").Delete
        CommandBars("Synoptics").Delete
        CommandBars("Project").Delete
End Sub
```

Program Special-key Use

Although many keys are reserved for Excel's use, many combinations of keys on the keyboard and the Alt, Shift, and Ctrl keys can be programmed to call routines. Below is the *Worksheet_Activate* function found on the MOD 2 EX worksheet object.

```
Sub Worksheet_Activate()
        Application.OnKey "%{g}",
"Generate_Necessary_Worksheets"
        Application.OnKey "%{pgup}", "Hide_UnHide_Sheets"
        Application.OnKey "%{pgdn}", "Hide_Sheets"
        Application.OnKey "%{home}", "Open_App"
        Application.OnKey "%{x}", "Close_App"
```

Application.OnKey "%{c}", "create_toolbars"
Application.OnKey "%{y}", "Hide_Command_Bars"
Application.OnKey "%{u}", "Unhide_Command_Bars"
Application.OnKey "%{end}", "Delete_Command_Bars"
Application.OnKey "%{q}", "Create_Comment"
   Application.StatusBar = "Cell comments indicate key
         commands to activate the associated functions"
End Sub

Before we launch into programming keys, let's point out the
Application.StatusBar statement at the bottom of the function.
That command tells Excel to replace any Excel status on the
command bar with text of our choosing. If we want to return
control of the status bar to Excel we use the
Application.StatusBar = False command.

The first command programs a combination of the Alt key (the
% symbol) and the G key to call the
Generate_Necessary_Worksheets function. To program a
combination of a keyboard key and the ctrl key the % symbol
would be replaced with a caret (^).. A Shift-key combination
would use the plus sign (+) .

As an example, if you wanted to use a combination of Shift, Ctrl,
and Alt plus the left- arrow key, the command would be:
   Application.OnKey "+^% {left}", "Do_Something"
Non-character key names:

Backspace	{backspace} or {bs}
Break	{break}
Caps Lock	{capslock}
Clear	{clear}
Delete or del	{delete} or {del}
Down arrow	{down}
End	{end}
Enter (numeric keypad}	{enter}
Enter	{~}
Esc	{escape} or {esc}
Help	{help}
Home	{home}
Ins	{insert}

Left arrow	{left}	
Num Lock	{numlock}	
Page Down	{pgdn}	
Page Up	{pgup}	
Return	{return}	
Right arrow	{right}	
Scroll Lock	{scrolllock}	
Tab	{tab}	
Up Arrow	{up}	
F1 through F15	{F1} through {F15}	

Determe the Number of Rows

The next two straightforward functions will be used mainly by other functions. The first will count rows in a column until it finds the first empty cell, and then it will stop and return to where it started. The bottom message box row is normally marked as a comment. If you want to run this routine alone and see the number of rows, remove the apostrophe from the final line.

```
Sub Determine_Rows()
    Row_Count = 0
    Do
        If ActiveCell > "" Then
            ActiveCell.Offset(1, 0).Select
            Row_Count = Row_Count + 1
        Else:
            ActiveCell.Offset(-Row_Count, 0).Select
            Exit Do
        End If
    Loop
    'MsgBox (Row_Count & "rows")
End Sub
```

Determine the Current Row

This routine will determine what row the currently selected cell is on, no matter which column is selected on that row.

```
Sub Determine_Current_Row()
    Point_1 = ActiveWindow.RangeSelection.Address
    Point_2 = Right(Point_1, Len(Point_1) - 1)
    For i = 1 To Len(Point_2)
        If Mid(Point_2, i, 1) = "$" Then
            Row = Right(Point_2, Len(Point_2) - i)
            Exit For
        End If
    Next i
    'MsgBox ("You are at Row " & Row)
End Sub
```

This routine includes a fairly useful command called
ActiveWindow.RangeSelection.Address. This command returns
the currently selected cell column and row location. As an
example, if the selected cell is F23, then the command would
return "F23." *Point_2* in the routine returns F$23. The
For/Next loop runs until the remaining "$" is found, and then
returns only the characters after it, in this case 23, which is the
row the selected cell is on.

The final Message Box command is marked as a comment
because this program is called by others. If you wish to run this
program alone and see which row you are on, then eliminate the
apostrophe.

Automatically Create Comments

This routine creates a comment in the selected cell. It also sets all
comments on the worksheet to the font size indicated in the *.Size*
parameter and makes them all bold. As it creates a new
comment, it leaves that new comment visible via the
ActiveCell.Comment.Visible = True statement.

```
Sub Create_Comment()
    'Automatic creation of comments*****************
    '{Alt+q} to run this routine
    ActiveCell.AddComment
    ActiveCell.Comment.Visible = True
```

```
        Cell_Comment = InputBox(Prompt:="Enter comment
            text", Title:="Cell Comment",
            Default:="Comment here")
        On Error GoTo Cancel_Comment
    ActiveCell.Comment.Text Text:=Cell_Comment
    ActiveCell.Comment.Shape.ScaleHeight 3.03, msoFalse,
    msoScaleFromTopLeft
    ActiveCell.Comment.Shape.ScaleWidth 2.33, msoFalse,
    msoScaleFromTopLeft
    ActiveCell.Comment.Shape.IncrementLeft -5.25
    ActiveCell.Comment.Shape.IncrementTop 46.5
    'Set all comments text size and make bold
    For Each com(should be caps?) In ActiveSheet.Comments
        With com.Shape
            .TextFrame.AutoSize = True
            .AutoShapeType = msoShapeRoundedRectangle
            With .TextFrame.Characters.Font
            .Size = 10
            .Bold = True
            End With
        End With
    Next com
: Cancel_Comment
End Sub
```

The *ActiveCell.Comment.Shape* statements set the comment box
size and location.

Create Shapes/Basic Drawing (Module 3)

In this section we are going to demonstrate how Microsoft Excel can be used as a drawing program. The *3* button on the *Project* toolbar will open the MOD 3 EX worksheet and perform the necessary initialization.

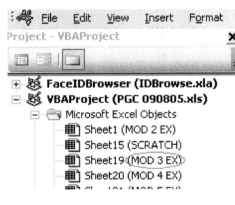

Select the MOD 3 EX worksheet object in the Visual Basic GUI to see the initialization code activated when the MOD 3 EX worksheet is selected.

All of the functions on this page are via special keys. To look up what those keys are press {Alt+Shift+?}. We've also programmed the status bar at the bottom of the screen to remind you of that fact.

Create a Block

We start with an extremely simple example. The routine below takes an area that has been highlighted and puts a border around it, which in effect creates a box.

```
Sub Make_a_Block()
    'Create a block***********************************
    Selection.Borders(xlDiagonalDown).LineStyle = xlNone
    Selection.Borders(xlDiagonalUp).LineStyle = xlNone
    With Selection.Borders(xlEdgeLeft)
        .LineStyle = xlContinuous
        .Weight = xlThick
        .ColorIndex = xlAutomatic
    End With
    With Selection.Borders(xlEdgeTop)
        .LineStyle = xlContinuous
        .Weight = xlThick
        .ColorIndex = xlAutomatic
```

End With
With Selection.Borders(xlEdgeBottom)
      .LineStyle = xlContinuous
      .Weight = xlThick
      .ColorIndex = xlAutomatic
End With
With Selection.Borders(xlEdgeRight)
      .LineStyle = xlContinuous
      .Weight = xlThick
      .ColorIndex = xlAutomatic
End With
With Selection.Interior
      .ColorIndex = 2
      .Pattern = xlSolid
      .PatternColorIndex = xlAutomatic
End With
Selection.Borders(xlInsideVertical).LineStyle = xlNone
Selection.Borders(xlInsideHorizontal).LineStyle = xlNone
ActiveCell.Offset(-2, 0).Select
   End Sub

Create a Triangle

This shape is still pretty straightforward. Using *For/Next* statements we build the three sides of the triangle. You select a cell and the triangle generated starts from that location.

Sub Make_a_Triangle()
  *'Create a triangle************************************
    'First, downward/forward slant side*
     For i = 1 To 4
         With Selection.Borders(xlDiagonalDown)
             .LineStyle = xlContinuous
             .Weight = xlThick
             .ColorIndex = xlAutomatic
         End With
         ActiveCell.Offset(1, 1).Select
     Next i
     ActiveCell.Offset(0, -1).Select
     'Second, downward/backward slant side

```
    For i = 1 To 4
        With Selection.Borders(xlDiagonalUp)
            .LineStyle = xlContinuous
            .Weight = xlThick
            .ColorIndex = xlAutomatic
        End With
        ActiveCell.Offset(1, -1).Select
    Next i
    ActiveCell.Offset(-1, 1).Select
    'Back side/vertical side
    For i = 1 To 8
        With Selection.Borders(xlEdgeLeft)
            .LineStyle = xlContinuous
            .Weight = xlThick
            .ColorIndex = xlAutomatic
        End With
        ActiveCell.Offset(-1, 0).Select
    Next i
End Sub
```

Create a Horizontal Line

This is another simple, straightforward function. Highlight the row area above where you want the line, and then run this function.

```
Sub Create_Horizontal_Line()
    'Create a horizontal line****************************
    With Selection.Borders(xlEdgeBottom)
        .LineStyle = xlContinuous
        .Weight = xlMedium
        .ColorIndex = xlAutomatic
    End With
End Sub
```

Create a Vertical Line

Creating a vertical line works exactly the same as the horizontal-line function above except you highlight the column area to the right of where you want your vertical line to be.

113

```
Sub Create_a_Vertical_Line()
    'Create a vertical line*******************************
    With Selection.Borders(xlEdgeLeft)
        .LineStyle = xlContinuous
        .Weight = xlMedium
        .ColorIndex = xlAutomatic
    End With
End Sub
```

Create a Special Character

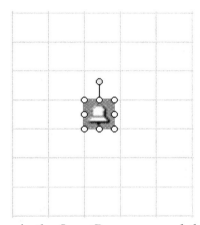

We can use Excel command bar icon objects in cells. Command bars are a class of Excel objects that comprise toolbars, menu bars, and shortcut menus. The routine below will add these icon objects into any cell selected. The icons are the same as the ones found in the *FaceID Browser* toolbar we mentioned earlier.

The routine generates a dialog box via the *InputBox* command that captures the user's character selection choice via the *Special_Character_No* variable.

```
Sub Create_Special_Character()
    Dim Special_Character_No As Integer
    Dim cbCtrl(should this be Ctrl?) As CommandBarControl
    Dim cbBar As CommandBar
    On Error GoTo No_Character
    Special_Character_No = InputBox(Prompt:="Save = 3"
        & Chr(10) & "Printer = 4" & Chr(10) & "Note =
        201" & Chr(10) & _
        "Magnifying Glass = 202" & Chr(10) & "Window
        Pane = 203" & Chr(10) & "Trapezoid = 206" &
        Chr(10) & _
```

"Design = 212" & Chr(10) & "Photo = 218" &
Chr(10) & "Check Mark = 220" & Chr(10) &
"Locked = 225" & Chr(10) & _
"Sum = 226" & Chr(10) & "SE Arrow = 243" &
Chr(10) & "Open Book = 247" & Chr(10) &
"Train Track = 251" & Chr(10) & _
"Excel = 263" & Chr(10) & "Key = 264" & Chr(10) &
"Musical Note = 272" & Chr(10) & "Bell = 273"
& Chr(10) & _
"Caption Balloon = 274" & Chr(10) & "Telephone =
275" & Chr(10) & "Unhappy Face = 276" &
Chr(10) & _
"Skeleton Key = 277" & Chr(10) & "Push Pin = 279"
& Chr(10) & "Push Button = 282" & Chr(10) &

_
"Calculator = 283" & Chr(10) & "Bar Chart = 284"
& Chr(10) & "Out of Stack = 292" & Chr(10) &

_
"Into Stack = 295" & Chr(10) & "Omega = 308" &
Chr(10) & "Not = 330" & Chr(10) & "LightBulb
! = 341" & Chr(10) & _
"Lightbulb White = 342" & Chr(10) & "Lightbulb
Yellow = 343" & Chr(10) & "Lightning Bolt =
346" & Chr(10) & _
"Right Arrow = 350" & Chr(10) & "Lightbulb Red =
352" & Chr(10) & "Up Arrow = 359" & Chr(10)
& _
"Down Arrow = 360" & Chr(10) & "White on Black
Arrow = 371" & Chr(10) & _
"White on Black Down Arrow = 372" & Chr(10) &
"White on Black Left Arrow = 373" & Chr(10) &

_
"! = 459", Title:="Select Special Character",
Default:="Enter Character #")
Set cbBar =
CommandBars.Add(Position:=msoBarFloating,
Menu Bar:=False, temporary:=True)
Set cbCtrl? =
cbBar.Controls.Add(Type:=msoControlButton,
temporary:=True)

cbCtrl?.FaceId = Special_Character_No
cbCtrl?.CopyFace
ActiveCell.PasteSpecial
Selection.ShapeRange.Fill.Visible = msoFalse
Selection.ShapeRange.Fill.Solid
Selection.ShapeRange.Fill.Transparency = 0#
Selection.ShapeRange.Line.Weight = 0#
Selection.ShapeRange.Line.DashStyle = msoLineSolid
Selection.ShapeRange.Line.Style = msoLineSingle
Selection.ShapeRange.Line.Transparency = 0#
Selection.ShapeRange.Line.Visible = msoTrue
Selection.ShapeRange.Line.ForeColor.SchemeColor = 10
Selection.ShapeRange.Line.BackColor.RGB = RGB(255, 255, 255)
No_Character:
End Sub

Create a Complex Line

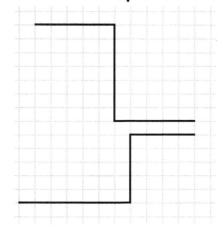

Often we would like to create a line that has more than one segment. The following routine allows you to create a three-segment line all at once. You select three points on a spreadsheet by holding the Ctrl key while selecting start, middle, and endpoints.

If the start and endpoints are on different rows, then the middle point determines where the second segment of the line travels vertically from the beginning row to the end row.

Add this sentence to the previous para.
Vertical travel from row to row can be up or down.

```
Sub Create_a_Complex_Line()
    Dim x As Integer
    On Error GoTo EndSub
    Route = ActiveWindow.RangeSelection.Address
    'Check for three points selected***************
    For i = 1 To Len(Route)
        If Mid(Route, i, 1) = "," Then
            x = 1
            Inn(what's this mean?Does it need
explanation?) = Right(Route, Len(Route) - i)
            Exit For
        End If
    Next i
    For i = 1 To Len(Inn)
        If Mid(Inn, i, 1) = "," Then
            Inn = Right(Inn, Len(Inn) - i)
            x = 2
            Exit For
        End If
    Next i
    If x <> 2 Then
        MsgBox ("Must Select 3 Points")
        Exit Sub
    End If
    For i = 1 To Len(Route)
        If Mid(Route, i, 1) = "," Then
            'Start Point**********
            Point_1 = Left(Route, (i - 1))
            Route = Right(Route, Len(Route) - i)
            Exit For
        End If
    Next i
    For i = 1 To Len(Route)
        If Mid(Route, i, 1) = "," Then
            'Midpoint**************
            Point_2 = Left(Route, (i - 1))
            'Endpoint***************
            Point_3 = Right(Route, Len(Route) - i)
            Exit For
        End If
```

```
Next i
'Start Col*************
Column_1 = Right(Point_1, (Len(Point_1) - 1))
For i = 1 To Len(Column_1)
    If Mid(Column_1, i, 1) = "$" Then
        Column_1 = Left(Column_1, (i - 1))
        'Start Row
        Row_1 = Right(Point_1, Len(Point_1) - (i + 1))
        Exit For
    End If
Next i
'Mid Col***************
Column_2 = Right(Point_2, (Len(Point_2) - 1))
For i = 1 To Len(Column_2)
    If Mid(Column_2, i, 1) = "$" Then
        Column_2 = Left(Column_2, (i - 1))
        'Mid Row
        Row_2 = Right(Point_2, Len(Point_2) - (i + 1))
        Exit For
    End If
Next i
'End Col**************
Column_3 = Right(Point_3, (Len(Point_3) - 1))
For i = 1 To Len(Column_3)
    If Mid(Column_3, i, 1) = "$" Then
        Column_3 = Left(Column_3, (i - 1))
        'End Row
        Row_3 = Right(Point_3, Len(Point_3) - (i + 1))
        Exit For
    End If
Next i
'******Done computing route column & row info*******
'Start Cell - Get Connector & Output Signal info*******
Range(Point_1).Select
'1st Line Segment******************
Line_Seg_1 = Column_1 & Row_1 & ":" & Column_2 &
Row_1
Range(Line_Seg_1).Select
With Selection.Borders(xlEdgeBottom)
    .LineStyle = xlContinuous
```

```
        .Weight = xlMedium
        .ColorIndex = xlAutomatic
    End With
    '2nd Line Segment*******************
    Line_Seg_2 = Column_2 & (Row_1 + 1) & ":" &
Column_2 & Row_3
    Range(Line_Seg_2).Select
    If Row_1 <> Row_3 Then
        With Selection.Borders(xlEdgeRight)
            .LineStyle = xlContinuous
            .Weight = xlMedium
            .ColorIndex = xlAutomatic
        End With
    End If
    If Row_1 > Row_3 Then
        Range(Column_2 & Row_3).Select
        Selection.Borders(xlEdgeRight).LineStyle = xlNone
        Range(Column_2 & (Row_1 + 1)).Select
        Selection.Borders(xlEdgeRight).LineStyle = xlNone
    End If
    '3rd Line Segment****************
    Line_Seg_3 = Column_2 & Row_3 & ":" & Column_3 &
Row_3
    Range(Line_Seg_3).Select
    With Selection.Borders(xlEdgeBottom)
        .LineStyle = xlContinuous
        .Weight = xlMedium
        .ColorIndex = xlAutomatic
    End With
    Range(Column_2 & Row_3).Select
    If Row_1 <> Row_3 Then
        Selection.Borders(xlEdgeBottom).LineStyle = xlNone
    End If
    Range(Column_3 & Row_3).Select
    Exit Sub
EndSub:
    MsgBox ("Sorry - Something has gone wrong")
End Sub
```

Seeing that this routine is a little more complex than most, it is annotated with more comments than most. As with most things, if we break this down into smaller parts it becomes much easier to understand.

Here we've selected three points by holding the Ctrl key and selecting the cells. The first point selected must be the left-most point; it is the start point. The second point selected determines where the line's vertical segment, if any, will be. The third and farthest right point will be the line's endpoint.

```
Sub Create_a_Complex_Line()
    Dim x As Integer
    On Error GoTo EndSub
    Route = ActiveWindow.RangeSelection.Address
Route = "$Q$6,$T$9,$X$10" } points selected***************
    For i = 1 To Len(Route)
        If Mid(Route, i, 1) = "," Then
```

The figure above shows that if the routine is paused at the first *For/Next* statement, the value of *Route* will be the locations of the three points. Here Q6 is the start point, T9 is the midpoint, and X10 is the endpoint.

The first two For/Next statements check to see if three points were selected by confirming that two commas are found in *Route*. The next two *For/Next* statements parse out or separate the three points into separate points (*Point_1/2/3*).

The next three *For/Next* statements separate out individual column and row values for each of the three points (*Column_1/2/3* and *Row_1/2/3*). Now, by using the *Row_1* value, and *Column_1* and *Column_2* values, we can create the first line segment. Using the *Column_2* value and *Row_1* and *Row_2* values, we create line segment two. Finally, using the *Row_3*

120

value and *Column_2* and *Column_3* values, we create the third line segment.

Notice that we check the value of *Row_1* versus *Row_3* three times. The first time, during the creation of line segment 2, is to see that *Row_1* is not equal to *Row_3*, which means a vertical line segment 2 is required. The second time during line segment two is to see whether line segment 2 travels up or down. If it travels up, then a couple end segments are erased.

The final time that the values of *Row_1* and *Row_3* are checked, to see if they are not equal (during line segment 3), is to trim the left end segment off line segment 3. If *Row_1* and *Row_3* are equal, it means that the three line segments form a single straight line and that piece of line segment 3 is needed.

Create Racks

Racks are metal enclosures in which equipment is placed. They can beused in many places, including in computer rooms, broadcast stations and telephone companies. If you haven't seen a rack, just think of them as shelves to store equipment. Below is an example from a television station, with racks of equipment on each side.

Often engineers will need to produce lists commonly known as rack elevations. These allow for the placement and management of equipment into available rack space. We have three routines that produce a row of rack elevations.

The first routine is the main routine and it calls the other two. The main routine asks for two values via Input Box commands. The first value it asks for is how many racks in a row. You can have up to 12 racks in a row due to column limitations imposed by Excel. The second value the routine asks for is the height of the rack. Rack height is not measured in inches, but in measurements called rack units(RUs)-, which are 1 ¾ in. tall.

Manufacturers design the height of rack-mountable gear to correspond to the RU. Racks generally measure 19in. wide from side to side, and come installed on? Missing a word here? front-mounting rails. In our program we make the space between rails 20 cells wide because some pieces of gear are only half the width of the rack space (or less), and 20 is divisible by 2. whereas 19 is not(at least, not as an even number).

```
'Racks & Frames///////////////////////////////////////////////////////////
Sub Rack_Elevation()
    Count = 0
    Rack = 1
    On Error GoTo Cancel_Racks
    Application.StatusBar = "      Rack Elevations (Max
    number in a row is 12)"
    Application.OnTime Now + TimeSerial(0, 0, 10),
    "ClearStatusBar"
        Racks = InputBox(Prompt:="Enter number of racks (max
            # 12)", Title:="Racks", Default:="# of racks")
        Height = InputBox(Prompt:="Enter height of racks",
            Title:="Rack Height", Default:="height of
            racks")
    Call Determine_Current_Row
    Range("A" & Row).Select
    ActiveCell.Offset(60, 0).Select
    Row = Row + 60
    For i = 1 To Racks
        Call Rack_Span
        Range(Col_1 & Row).Select
        Call Construct_Rack
        Rack = Rack + 1
    Next i
    Cancel_Racks:
End Sub
```

In this first main routine, the first part of the program gathers the two previously mentioned pieces of information, determines what row you are currently on, and then jumps down 60 rows to the bottom of where the row of racks will be.

A *For/Next* statement is then used to produce the number of racks desired in the row. In the *For/Next* loop, two other routines are called to actually construct the rack.

The first routine (*Rack_Span*) determines what columns on the worksheet that the left and right sides of the rack will occupy. It does that based on the value of *Rack*. The value of *Rack* is increased by one as each loop through the *For/Next* loop is run. *Rack_Span* is the second routine down from here.

The routine that actually constructs the rack is the one immediately below. The comments inside the routine point out where each side of the rack construction begins.

```
Sub Construct_Rack()
    Rack_Anchor = ActiveWindow.RangeSelection.Address
    ActiveCell = Rack
    Range(Rack_Anchor).Select
    'Create rack base
    Range_Select = Col_2 & (Row + 1)
    Range(Rack_Anchor & ":" & Range_Select).Select
    With Selection.Interior
        .ColorIndex = 1
        .Pattern = xlSolid
        .PatternColorIndex = xlAutomatic
    End With
    Range(Rack_Anchor).Select
    'Left rack side
    ActiveCell.Offset(-1, 0).Select
    For i = 1 To Height
        With Selection.Interior
            .ColorIndex = 1
            .Pattern = xlSolid
            .PatternColorIndex = xlAutomatic
        End With
        ActiveCell = i
        With Selection
            .HorizontalAlignment = xlRight
            .VerticalAlignment = xlBottom
        End With
```

```
With Selection.Font
        .Name = "Arial"
        .FontStyle = "Regular"
        .Size = 8
        .Strikethrough = False
        .Superscript = False
        .Subscript = False
        .OutlineFont = False
        .Shadow = False
        .Underline = xlUnderlineStyleNone
        .ColorIndex = 2
    End With
    ActiveCell.Offset(-1, 0).Select
Next i
'Top of Rack
Row = Row - (Height + 1)
Range_Select = Col_1 & Row & ":" & Col_2 & Row
Range(Range_Select).Select
With Selection.Interior
    .ColorIndex = 1
    .Pattern = xlSolid
    .PatternColorIndex = xlAutomatic
End With
Range(Col_1 & Row).Select
ActiveCell.Offset(0, 9).Select
ActiveCell = Rack_S
With Selection
    .HorizontalAlignment = xlCenter
    .VerticalAlignment = xlBottom
End With
With Selection.Font
    .Name = "Arial"
    .FontStyle = "Regular"
    .Size = 10
    .Strikethrough = False
    .Superscript = False
    .Subscript = False
    .OutlineFont = False
    .Shadow = False
    .Underline = xlUnderlineStyleNone
```

```
                .ColorIndex = 2
        End With
        'Right Rack Side
        Range(Col_2 & Row).Select
        For i = 1 To (Height + 1)
                Row = Row + 1
                With Selection.Interior
                        .ColorIndex = 1
                        .Pattern = xlSolid
                        .PatternColorIndex = xlAutomatic
                End With
                ActiveCell.Offset(1, 0).Select
        Next i
        Range(Rack_Anchor).Select
End Sub

Sub Rack_Span()
        Select Case Rack
                Case Is = 1
                        Col_1 = "B"
                        Col_2 = "V"
                Case Is = 2
                        Col_1 = "W"
                        Col_2 = "AQ"
                Case Is = 3
                        Col_1 = "AR"
                        Col_2 = "BL"
                Case Is = 4
                        Col_1 = "BM"
                        Col_2 = "CG"
                Case Is = 5
                        Col_1 = "CH"
                        Col_2 = "DB"
                Case Is = 6
                        Col_1 = "DC"
                        Col_2 = "DW"
                Case Is = 7
                        Col_1 = "DX"
                        Col_2 = "ER"
                Case Is = 8
```

126

```
        Col_1 = "ES"
        Col_2 = "FM"
   Case Is = 9
        Col_1 = "FN"
        Col_2 = "GH"
   Case Is = 10
        Col_1 = "GI"
        Col_2 = "HC"
   Case Is = 11
        Col_1 = "HD"
        Col_2 = "HX"
   Case Is = 12
        Col_1 = "HY"
        Col_2 = "IS"
  End Select
End Sub
```

You can now use the box-creation routines we developed earlier to fill in the rack with equipment. See below for an example of automatically generated racks. The *create-a-box* routine was used to depict equipment in the second rack.

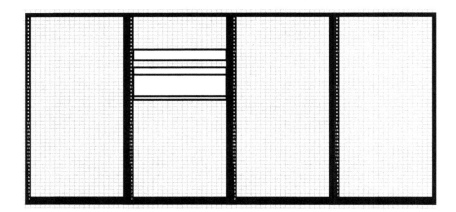

127

Clear Area Selected

Finally, to help erase lines, blocks, and racks quickly and easily we have one final routine in the Drawing section. We use cell borders to create the various lines and boxes in our drawings. This straightforward routine simply erases all borders and characters, and clears all selected cells of fill patterns.

Sub Clear_Area_Selected()

    Selection.Borders(xlDiagonalDown).LineStyle = xlNone
    Selection.Borders(xlDiagonalUp).LineStyle = xlNone
    Selection.Borders(xlEdgeLeft).LineStyle = xlNone
    Selection.Borders(xlEdgeTop).LineStyle = xlNone
    Selection.Borders(xlEdgeBottom).LineStyle = xlNone
    Selection.Borders(xlEdgeRight).LineStyle = xlNone
    Selection.Borders(xlInsideVertical).LineStyle = xlNone
    Selection.Borders(xlInsideHorizontal).LineStyle = xlNone
    Selection.Interior.ColorIndex = xlNone
    Selection.ClearContents

End Sub

Calculations--Finance (Module 4)

In this section we will look at using VBA to compute financial amounts. Although Excel has many built-in math, finance, and other calculation tools, they need to be embedded into cells and, as such, can be easily changed or damaged. Using VBA you can have any cell hold the result of a calculation, and any manipulation of that cell will not result in the inability of VBA to compute a desired value in the future.

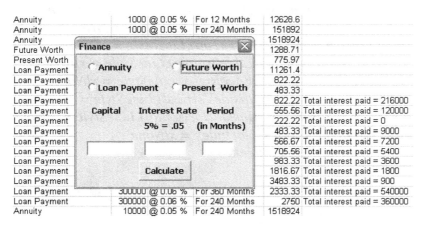

When worksheet MOD 4 EX is selected, the above user form is displayed. By selecting one of the four calculation choices, the user can run the routines below to calculate values based on his or her input.

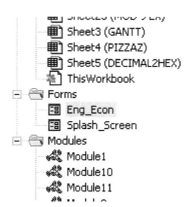

To call the routines the user form, shown and highlighted to the left, contains code that prompts for various variables based on what calculation is to be performed.

By selecting the *Eng_Econ* user form and then right clicking on any blank area of the form, you can choose to view code on the form.

129

Here are the routines that are part of the *Eng_Econ* user form object. The routines all have the ending *_Click* automatically addedby Excel). There is one for each object on the user form. The "Private" at the head of each routine indicates that these routines can be called only by this user form, not by outside modules.

This routine is invoked each time you click the radio button associated with the *Annuity* button. The *Case_Selection* variable is used when the *Calculate* button is selected. *Eng_Econ.Amount_Text* changes the text over the left-most textbox on the user form.

```
Private Sub Annu_Click()
    Case_Selection = "Annuity"
    Eng_Econ.Amount_Text = "Desired Annual Income"
End Sub
```

This is the main routine on the user form. It is run whenever the *Calculate* button is selected. The *Case_Selection* value is set via the *Annuity*, *Future Worth*, *Loan Payment*, and *Present Worth* radio-button routines. The various associated routines are called based on the Case_Selection value.

```
Private Sub Calculate_Click()
    On Error GoTo Calc_Error
    Call Clear_Eng_Econ
    Cash = Eng_Econ.Cash_Amount
    Interest = Eng_Econ.Interest_Rate
    Interest2 = (Interest / 12)
    Period = Eng_Econ.Period_Mo
    Select Case Case_Selection
        Case Is = "Annuity"
            Call Calc_Annuity
        Case Is = "Future Worth"
            Call Calculate_Future_Worth
        Case Is = "Loan Payment"
            Call Calculate_Loan_Payment
        Case Is = "Present Worth"
            Call Calculate_Present_Worth
    End Select
```

Calc_Error:
End Sub

These are the other three calculation choice buttons. Excel automatically places the routines in alphabetical order when creating them for user forms, but not for normal modules.

Private Sub FW_Click()
*   Case_Selection = "Future Worth"*
*   Eng_Econ.Amount_Text = "Starting Amount"*
End Sub

Private Sub Loan_Click()
*   Case_Selection = "Loan Payment"*
*   Eng_Econ.Amount_Text = "Loan Principle"*
End Sub

Private Sub PW_Click()
*   Case_Selection = "Present Worth"*
*   Eng_Econ.Amount_Text = "Future Amount"*
End Sub

Starting here are the finance routines in Module 4. We usually place them in the same order as you will find them on the module, but in this case, we have grouped *Clear_Eng_Econ* with , *Calc_Compound_Amount* and *Print_Results*at the bottom of Module 4, as these three are common to most of the other routines.

Clear_Eng_Econ simply clears the user form. It is called whenever *Calculate_Click* is run.

Sub Clear_Eng_Econ()
*   'Finance**
*   Dim ctrl? As Control*
*   For Each ctrl? In Eng_Econ.Controls*
*   If TypeName(ctrl?) = "OptionButton" Then*
*   ctrl?.Value = False*
*   End If*
*   Next ctrl?*
End Sub

This routine is used by three of the four calculation routines; only *Calculate_Loan_Payment* does not call it. It performs the task that a mathematical series would perform; it literally compounds the *Compound_Amount* value based on how many periods the calculation covers. Because everything is compounded on a monthly basis, the *Interest2* value is simply the yearly interest rate divided by 12.

```
Sub Calc_Compound_Amount()
    'Finance*****************************************
    Compound_Amount = 1 + Interest2
    For i = 1 To Period
        Compound_Amount = Compound_Amount * (1 +
        Interest2)
    Next i
End Sub
```

This routine records the results of a calculation on the MOD 4 EX worksheet as shown before. The routine finds the next available blank line and prints the results.

```
Sub Print_Results()
    'Finance*****************************************
    'Find next available line
    Total = Round(Total, 2)
    Sheets("MOD 4 EX").Select
    Range("A1").Select
    Do
        If ActiveCell = "" Then
            ActiveCell = Case_Selection
            ActiveCell.Offset(0, 1).Select
            ActiveCell = Cash
            ActiveCell.Offset(0, 1).Select
            ActiveCell = "@ " & Interest & " %"
            ActiveCell.Offset(0, 1).Select
            ActiveCell = "For " & Period & " Months"
            ActiveCell.Offset(0, 1).Select
            ActiveCell = Total
            Exit Do
        Else:
            ActiveCell.Offset(1, 0).Select
        End If
    Loop
End Sub
```

Calculate an Annuity

The routine does as it name implies--it calculates an annuity based upon the desiredmonthly return, the interest rate, and how many months ofpayout.

```
Sub Calc_Annuity()
    'Sub Calculate an annuity**************************
    Dim Account_Balance As Double
    Call Calc_Compound_Amount
      Account_Balance = Cash * (Compound_Amount - 1) /
            (Interest2 * Compound_Amount)
    Total = Account_Balance
    Call Print_Results
End Sub
```

Calculate the Future Worth of a Sum of Money

This routine takes a present sum of cash, and based on the interest rate and over how many months you want to compound the interest, it tells you what the sum will be at the end.

```
Sub Calculate_Future_Worth()
    'Calculate future worth of a sum of money************
    Dim Future_Worth As Double
    Call Calc_Compound_Amount
    Future_Worth = Cash * Compound_Amount
    Total = Future_Worth
    Call Print_Results
End Sub
```

Calculate the Present Worth of a Future Sum of Money

This routine does the opposite of *Calculate_Future_Worth*. You enter the amount of money you want to have after a given number of months, and it tells you what you need to invest today.

```
Sub Calculate_Present_Worth()
     Dim Present_Worth As Double
     Call Calc_Compound_Amount
     Compound_Amount = 1 / Compound_Amount
     Present_Worth = Cash * Compound_Amount
     Total = Present_Worth
     Call Print_Results
End Sub
```

Calculate a Loan Payment

Again this routine does what it says: it calculates a loan payment. You provide the loan principle and interest rate, and over how many months you want to pay the loan off, and it computes your monthly payment. This routine adds one other piece of information after the information that *Print_Results* provides. It tells you how much interest you paid over the course of the loan.

```
Sub Calculate_Loan_Payment()
     'Calculate a loan
payment****************************
     Dim Loan_Payment As Double
     Dim Total_Interest As Double
     Call Calc_Compound_Amount
     Total_Interest = Cash * (Period * Interest2)
     Total = Cash + Total_Interest
     Loan_Payment = Total / Period
     Total = Loan_Payment
     Call Print_Results
     ActiveCell.Offset(0, 1).Select
     ActiveCell = "Total interest paid = " & Total_Interest
End Sub
```

Timelines/Project Planning (Module 5)

Now let's look at how we can use Microsoft Excel to generate a simple project timeline, much like a Gantt chart thatpresents the tasks to be completed and where they fit into the overall project timeline.

Generate a Timeline for a Project

At the top of our chart we want to create dates that correspond to the length of time that our project will span. The second routine will list every seventh date across the top of the chart. These dates should correspond to the Monday of each week of the project span.

```
Sub Select_Start_End_Dates()
    'Generate a timeline for a project*******************
    On Error GoTo Exit_Dates_Sub
    Start_Date = InputBox(Prompt:="Enter Monday before
    project start", _
        Title:="Start Date", Default:=Date)
    End_Date = InputBox(Prompt:="Enter End Date of
    project", _
        Title:="End Date", Default:=Date + 7)
    Call Create_Project_Timeline
Exit_Dates_Sub:
End Sub

Sub Create_Project_Timeline()
    'Generate a timeline for a project*******************
    Count = 1
    Dim Monday As Date
    Monday = Start_Date
    Rows("1:1").Select
    Selection.ClearContents
    Range("A1").Select
    ActiveCell = Start_Date
    Do
        Count = Count + 7
        If Count > 255 Then
        MsgBox ("End date out of range!" & Chr(10) & _
```

```
                    "Worksheet can only handle 36 weeks")
            Exit Do
        End If
        ActiveCell.Offset(0, 7).Select
        Monday = Monday + 7
        If Monday > End_Date Then
            ActiveCell = Monday
            Exit Do
        End If
        ActiveCell = Monday
    Loop
    Range("A1").Select
End Sub
```

List Project Steps

This routine creates a list of project steps from the SCRATCH worksheet starting at cell G1 and transfers them with blank start-stop dates to the MOD 5 EX worksheet.

```
Sub List_Tasks()
    'Generate a Gantt Chart**************************
    Gantt_Form_Enabled = False
    Sheets("MOD 5 EX").Select
    Rows("2:2000").Select
    Selection.ClearContents
    Selection.Interior.ColorIndex = xlNone
    Range("A3").Select
    Sheets("SCRATCH").Visible = True
    Sheets("SCRATCH").Select
    Range("G1").Select
    If ActiveCell = "" Then
        MsgBox ("List of project steps starts at G1 on the
        SCRATCH worksheet")
    End If
    Call Determine_Rows
    For i = 1 To Row_Count
        ActiveCell = UCase(ActiveCell)
        Sheet_Name = ActiveCell
```

```
        ActiveCell.Offset(1, 0).Select
        Sheets("MOD 5 EX").Select
        ActiveCell = Sheet_Name
        ActiveCell.Offset(0, 20).Select
        ActiveCell = "START"
        ActiveCell.Offset(0, 5).Select
        ActiveCell = "END"
        ActiveCell.Offset(3, -25).Select
        Sheets("SCRATCH").Select
    Next i
    Sheets("MOD 5 EX").Select
    Range("A4").Select
    Gantt_Form_Enabled = True
End Sub
```

Save Project Dates

Once the List_Tasks routine above has listed each step on your project chart, you need to replace the Start/Stop cells with actual project start and stop dates for each step. Once you've entered these dates, this routine will store those dates in Column J (start date) and column K (end date) on the SCRATCH worksheet.

```
Sub Save_Dates()
    'Save project dates*********************************
    Gantt_Form_Enabled = False
    Sheets("SCRATCH").Visible = True
    Sheets("SCRATCH").Select
    Range("G1:L100").Select
    Selection.ClearContents
    Range("G1").Select
    Sheets("MOD 5 EX").Select
    Range("A3").Select
    Do
        If ActiveCell = "" Then
            Exit Do
        End If
        Sheet_Name = ActiveCell
        ActiveCell.Offset(0, 20).Select
```

```
        If ActiveCell = "START" Then
                Start_Date = Date
        Else:
                Start_Date = ActiveCell
        End If
        ActiveCell.Offset(0, 5).Select
        If ActiveCell = "END" Then
                End_Date = Date + 7
        Else:
                End_Date = ActiveCell
        End If
        ActiveCell.Offset(3, -25).Select
        Sheets("SCRATCH").Select
        ActiveCell = Sheet_Name
        ActiveCell.Offset(0, 3).Select
        ActiveCell = Start_Date
        ActiveCell.Offset(0, 1).Select
        ActiveCell = End_Date
        ActiveCell.Offset(1, -4).Select
        Sheets("MOD 5 EX").Select
    Loop
    Gantt_Form_Enabled = True
    Sheets("MOD 5 EX").Select
End Sub
```

Recall Project Dates

This routine does the opposite of the routine above. It pulls the dates off columns J and K on the SCRATCH worksheet and associates them with the proper listed project steps on your project timeline (worksheet MOD 5 EX).

```
Sub Recall_Previous_Dates()
        'Recall project dates*******************************
        Gantt_Form_Enabled = False
        Sheets("MOD 5 EX").Select
        Range("U2:Z300").Select
        Selection.ClearContents
        Sheets("SCRATCH").Visible = True
```

138

```
Sheets("SCRATCH").Select
Range("G1").Select
Call Determine_Rows
For i = 1 To Row_Count
        Start_Date = 0
        End_Date = 0
        Sheet_Name = ActiveCell
        ActiveCell.Offset(0, 3).Select
        Start_Date = ActiveCell
        ActiveCell.Offset(0, 1).Select
        End_Date = ActiveCell
        ActiveCell.Offset(1, -4).Select
        If Start_Date <> "12:00:00 AM" Then
                Sheets("MOD 5 EX").Select
                Range("A3").Select
                Do
                        If ActiveCell = Sheet_Name Then
                                ActiveCell.Offset(0, 20).Select
                                ActiveCell = Start_Date
                                ActiveCell.Offset(0, 5).Select
                                ActiveCell = End_Date
                                ActiveCell.Offset(3, -25).Select
                                Exit Do
                        Else:
                                ActiveCell.Offset(3, 0).Select
                        End If
                        If ActiveCell = "" Then
                                Exit Do
                        End If
                Loop
        End If
        Sheets("SCRATCH").Select
    Next i
    Sheets("MOD 5 EX").Select
    Gantt_Form_Enabled = True
End Sub
```

Generate Gantt chart Timelines

This routine looks at the start/end dates associated with each step and creates a bar under each step indicating how many days a particular step will occupy.

```
Sub Create_Time_lines()
    'Generate a Gantt Chart***************************
    On Error Resume Next
    Dim Monday As Date
    Dim Date_Offset As Integer
    Dim Run_Length As Integer
    Count = 0
    Gantt_Form_Enabled = False
    Sheets("MOD 5 EX").Select
    Range("A1").Select
    Monday = ActiveCell
    Range("U3").Select
    Do
        If ActiveCell > 0 Then
            Start_Date = ActiveCell
            Point_1 =
            ActiveWindow.RangeSelection.Address
            ActiveCell.Offset(0, 5).Select
            End_Date = ActiveCell
            If End_Date = 0 Then
                ActiveCell.Offset(3, -5).Select
            Else:
                ActiveCell.Offset(1, -25).Select
                For i = 1 To 255
                        Selection.Interior.ColorIndex =
                        xlNone
                        ActiveCell.Offset(0, 1).Select
                Next i
                ActiveCell.Offset(0, -255).Select
                Date_Offset = Start_Date - Monday
                ActiveCell.Offset(0, Date_Offset).Select
                Run_Length = End_Date - Start_Date
                For i = 1 To Run_Length
                        Selection.Interior.ColorIndex = 15
```

```
                         ActiveCell.Offset(0, 1).Select
                Next i
                Range(Point_1).Select
                ActiveCell.Offset(3, 0).Select
              End If
        Else:
                ActiveCell.Offset(3, 0).Select
                Count = Count + 1
          End If
          If Count > 50 Then
                Range("A4").Select
                Exit Do
          End If
      Loop
      Sheets("MOD 5 EX").Select
      Gantt_Form_Enabled = True
      Sheets("SCRATCH").Visible = False
End Sub
```

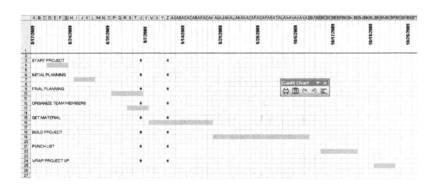

This is what the finished result looks like on sheet MOD 5 EX.
The values in the U and Z columns are the start and end times
you entered, which are used to create the duration bar graphs.

2D Color Drawing/Generate a Floor Plan

Ready the Floor Plan

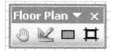

Select the hand icon on the *Floor Plan* toolbar to run the *Make_Floor_Plan_Ready* routine.

This routine simply puts the legend in the upper-left corner of the spreadsheet. The routine also calls the *Room_Colors* routine, which creates the colored cells and the legend for each color. The various colors correspond to rooms within the facility. Here we use room labels that might be found in a television broadcast facility.

```
Sub Make_Floor_Plan_Ready()
    Floor_Plan_Enabled = False
    Range("A1").Select
    ActiveCell = "1 square = 1 sq ft"
    Selection.Font.Bold = True
    With Selection.Font
        .Name = "Arial"
        .Size = 12
        .Strikethrough = False
        .Superscript = False
        .Subscript = False
        .OutlineFont = False
        .Shadow = False
        .Underline = xlUnderlineStyleNone
        .ColorIndex = xlAutomatic
    End With
    ActiveCell.Offset(1, 0).Select
    ActiveCell.Offset(1, 0).Select
    Call Room_Colors
    Floor_?Plan_Enabled = True
End Sub
```

142

Color-code Rooms

Sub Room_Colors()
    Range("A3").Select
    Selection.Interior.ColorIndex = 40
    ActiveCell.Offset(0, 1).Select
    ActiveCell = "PCR 1"
    ActiveCell.Offset(1, -1).Select
    Selection.Interior.ColorIndex = 38
    ActiveCell.Offset(0, 1).Select
    ActiveCell = "PCR 2"
    ActiveCell.Offset(1, -1).Select
    Selection.Interior.ColorIndex = 36
    ActiveCell.Offset(0, 1).Select
    ActiveCell = "Audio"
    ActiveCell.Offset(1, -1).Select
    Selection.Interior.ColorIndex = 35
    ActiveCell.Offset(0, 1).Select
    ActiveCell = "VTR/Storage"
    ActiveCell.Offset(1, -1).Select
    Selection.Interior.ColorIndex = 34
    ActiveCell.Offset(0, 1).Select
    ActiveCell = "Engineering"
    ActiveCell.Offset(1, -1).Select
    Selection.Interior.ColorIndex = 37
    ActiveCell.Offset(0, 1).Select
    ActiveCell = "Video"
    ActiveCell.Offset(1, -1).Select
    Selection.Interior.ColorIndex = 39
    ActiveCell.Offset(0, 1).Select
    ActiveCell = "MCR/Release"
    ActiveCell.Offset(1, -1).Select
    Selection.Interior.ColorIndex = 44
    ActiveCell.Offset(0, 1).Select
    ActiveCell = "Acquisition"
    ActiveCell.Offset(1, -1).Select
    Selection.Interior.ColorIndex = 6
    ActiveCell.Offset(0, 1).Select
    ActiveCell = "Transmission"

```
    ActiveCell.Offset(1, -1).Select
    Selection.Interior.ColorIndex = 43
    ActiveCell.Offset(0, 1).Select
    ActiveCell = "Misc"
    ActiveCell.Offset(1, -1).Select
End Sub
```

Create a Facility (or Home) layout

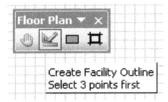

The drafting icon on the *Floor Plan* toolbar is used to create the outline of your overall facility or building. When you hold the mouse over the icon, you will be prompted to enter three points. Do this by holding the Ctrl key while selecting the points.

If you have a facility that is not square, you can simply overlap square spaces and erase the interior borders to create a complex space.

The *Make_Facility* function is a stand-alone function. This function requires that you select three points. Select one point, and then while holding the Ctrl key, select two others. The first point represents the upper-left corner, the second anywhere along the right edge, and the third anywhere along the bottom edge. These three points are stored in the variable *Boundry* once the function starts.

Top_Left, *Top_Right*, and *Bottom* points are parsed out of *Boundry* in the first two sets of *For/Next* statements. The next three *For/Next* statements further parse out sets of *Row_1/Col_1*, *Row_2/Col_2*, and *Row_3/Col_3* values. From these, *Point_1/2/3* values are created, representing the upper-left, upper-right, and lower-right points. The fourth point is created using a combination of *Point 3* and *Col_1* and *Row_3*. These four points are connected by *Range* statements with thick borders to create a four-sided rectangle.

Sub Make_Facility( )
    Dim x As Integer
    Dim temp As String
    Sheets("MOD 6 EX").Select
    Boundry = ActiveWindow.RangeSelection.Address
    'Check for three points selected
    For i = 1 To Len(Boundry)

```
        If Mid(Boundry, i, 1) = "," Then
                x = 1
                Top_Left = Left(Boundry, i - 1)
                Boundry = Right(Boundry, Len(Boundry) - i)
                Exit For
        End If
Next i
For i = 1 To Len(Boundry)
        If Mid(Boundry, i, 1) = "," Then
                x = 2
                Top_Right = Left(Boundry, i - 1)
                Bottom = Right(Boundry, Len(Boundry) - i)
                If Bottom > "" Then
                    x = 3
                End If
                Exit For
        End If
Next i
If x < 3 Then
        MsgBox ("Must Select 3 Points")
        Exit Sub
End If
Col_1 = Right(Top_Left, Len(Top_Left) - 1)
For i = 1 To Len(Col_1)
        If Mid(Col_1, i, 1) = "$" Then
                Row_1 = Right(Col_1, Len(Col_1) - i)
                Col_1 = Left(Col_1, (i - 1))
                Exit For
        End If
Next i
Point_1 = Col_1 & Row_1
Col_2 = Right(Top_Right, Len(Top_Right) - 1)
For i = 1 To Len(Col_2)
        If Mid(Col_2, i, 1) = "$" Then
                Row_2 = Right(Col_2, Len(Col_2) - i)
                Col_2 = Left(Col_2, (i - 1))
                Exit For
        End If
Next i
Point_2 = Col_2 & Row_1
```

```
Col_3 = Right(Bottom, Len(Bottom) - 1)
For i = 1 To Len(Col_3)
        If Mid(Col_3, i, 1) = "$" Then
                Row_3 = Right(Col_3, Len(Col_3) - i)
                Col_3 = Left(Col_3, (i - 1))
                Exit For
        End If
Next i
Point_3 = Col_2 & Row_3
Range(Point_1 & ":" & Point_2).Select
With Selection.Borders(xlEdgeTop)
        .LineStyle = xlContinuous
        .Weight = xlThick
        .ColorIndex = xlAutomatic
End With
Range(Point_2 & ":" & Point_3).Select
With Selection.Borders(xlEdgeRight)
        .LineStyle = xlContinuous
        .Weight = xlThick
        .ColorIndex = xlAutomatic
End With
Range(Point_3 & ":" & Col_1 & Row_3).Select
With Selection.Borders(xlEdgeBottom)
        .LineStyle = xlContinuous
        .Weight = xlThick
        .ColorIndex = xlAutomatic
End With
Range(Col_1 & Row_3 & ":" & Point_1).Select
With Selection.Borders(xlEdgeLeft)
        .LineStyle = xlContinuous
        .Weight = xlThick
        .ColorIndex = xlAutomatic
End With
ActiveCell.Offset(2, 0).Select
End Sub
```

Create a Room

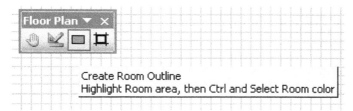

Create Room Outline
Highlight Room area, then Ctrl and Select Room color

We purposely made this function work differently from the *Make_Facility* function.

Here the room area is highlighted via a drag-and-drop motion, and then Ctrl is held while the desired room color is selected.

The bulk of the work in this function is done by the following function: *Determine_Area_and_A_Point*. The rest of this function simply outlines the selected room area (*Point_1* and *Point_2*) with a thick border and labels the room; the point containing the room color is parsed out in *Determine_Area_and_A_Point*.

Sub Make_Room()
     Call Determine_Area_and_A_Point
     Range(Point_3).Select
     Color = Selection.Interior.ColorIndex
     ActiveCell.Offset(0, 1).Select
     Room = ActiveCell
     'Make Room
     Range(Point_1 & ":" & Point_2).Select
     With Selection.Borders(xlEdgeLeft)
          .LineStyle = xlContinuous
          .Weight = xlThick
          .ColorIndex = xlAutomatic
     End With
     With Selection.Borders(xlEdgeTop)
          .LineStyle = xlContinuous
          .Weight = xlThick
          .ColorIndex = xlAutomatic
     End With

```
With Selection.Borders(xlEdgeBottom)
     .LineStyle = xlContinuous
     .Weight = xlThick
     .ColorIndex = xlAutomatic
End With
With Selection.Borders(xlEdgeRight)
     .LineStyle = xlContinuous
     .Weight = xlThick
     .ColorIndex = xlAutomatic
End With
'Fill in room color
With Selection.Interior
     .ColorIndex = Color
     .Pattern = xlSolid
     .PatternColorIndex = xlAutomatic
End With
Range(Point_1).Select
ActiveCell = Room
Floor_OK?Plan_Enabled = True
End Sub
```

The variable *Boundry* contains the upper-left and lower-right
points selected for the room, and a third point, which is the cell
location of the room color selected. The first two *For/Next*
statements parse out *Point_1/2/3* into the separate points from
the *Boundry* variable. At this point, the points still have $
symbols in them. The next three For/Next statements eliminate
the $.

```
Sub Determine_Area_and_A_Point()
     Dim x As Integer
     Dim temp As String
     Sheets("MOD 6 EX").Select
     Boundry = ActiveWindow.RangeSelection.Address
     'Check for three points selected
     For i = 1 To Len(Boundry)
          If Mid(Boundry, i, 1) = ":" Then
               x = 1
               Point_1 = Left(Boundry, i - 1)
               Boundry = Right(Boundry, Len(Boundry) - i)
```

```
                    Exit For
            End If
    Next i
    For i = 1 To Len(Boundry)
        If Mid(Boundry, i, 1) = "," Then
                x = 2
                Point_2 = Left(Boundry, i - 1)
                Point_3 = Right(Boundry, Len(Boundry) - i)
                If Point_3 > "" Then
                    x = 3
                End If
                Exit For
        End If
    Next i
    If x < 3 Then
        MsgBox ("Must select area and then select a 3rd
        point")
        Exit Sub
    End If
    Point_1 = Right(Point_1, Len(Point_1) - 1)
    For i = 1 To Len(Point_1)
        If Mid(Point_1, i, 1) <> "$" Then
                temp = temp & Mid(Point_1, i, 1)
        Else:
                Top_Left = Right(Point_1, Len(Point_1) - i)
        End If
    Next i
    Point_1 = temp
     temp = ""
    Point_2 = Right(Point_2, Len(Point_2) - 1)
    For i = 1 To Len(Point_2)
        If Mid(Point_2, i, 1) <> "$" Then
                temp = temp & Mid(Point_2, i, 1)
        Else:
                Bottom = Right(Point_2, Len(Point_2) - i)
        End If
    Next i
    Point_2 = temp
    temp = ""
    Col_1 = ""
```

```
        Point_3 = Right(Point_3, Len(Point_3) - 1)
        For i = 1 To Len(Point_3)
            If Mid(Point_3, i, 1) <> "$" Then
                    temp = temp & Mid(Point_3, i, 1)
            Else:
                    Col_1 = temp
            End If
        Next i
        Point_3 = temp
End Sub
```

Add Objects to the Room

This is a stand-alone function. The *Boundry* variable contains
upper-left and lower-right points of area highlighted for racks.
Racks can run either east-west or north-south. Rows of racks
must measure only two cells wide. The variable *Boundry*
contains the upper-left and lower-right points that denote the row
of racks for a facility, but the variable could be modified to allow
for furniture in a home or office.

The first three *For/Next* statements separate the two points into
individual rows and columns for each point. The next four *With*
statements outline the row of racks. The next two *With*
statements make vertical and horizontal borders inside the
outlined area.

Now it is determined whether the row is running vertically
(north-south) or horizontally (east-west) by seeing whether
between *Row_A* and *Row_B* is greater than one (if so, then the
row is running vertically).

If the rows are running horizontally, then every other vertical and
center horizontal border is eliminated on the bottom row with the
first *Do* loop. If an extra column is encountered (*Row_Count* =
2) meaning that a half rack more is found, then that half rack
extra is eliminated. Then the top row of every other vertical
border and remaining center horizontal border is eliminated with
the second *Do* loop, creating a row of two-cell-by-two-cell racks.

Similar procedure is followed for vertical rack orientation.

```
Sub Make_Racks()
    Dim x As Integer
    Dim y As Integer
    Dim z As Integer
    Dim temp As String
    Count = 0
    Dim iReply As Integer
    Dim oddval As Variant
    Horizontal = False
    Vertical = False
    On Error GoTo ErrorHandler
    Sheets("MOD 6 EX").Select
    Boundry = ActiveWindow.RangeSelection.Address
    Col_1 = Right(Boundry, Len(Boundry) - 1)
    For i = 1 To Len(Col_1)
        If Mid(Col_1, i, 1) = "$" Then
            Row_A = Right(Col_1, Len(Col_1) - i)
            Col_1 = Left(Col_1, (i - 1))
            Exit For
        End If
    Next i
    For i = 1 To Len(Row_A)
        If Mid(Row_A, i, 1) = ":" Then
            Col_2 = Right(Row_A, Len(Row_A) - (i + 1))
            Row_A = Left(Row_A, (i - 1))
            Exit For
        End If
    Next i
    For i = 1 To Len(Col_2)
        If Mid(Col_2, i, 1) = "$" Then
            Row_B = Right(Col_2, Len(Col_2) - i)
            Col_2 = Left(Col_2, (i - 1))
            Exit For
        End If
    Next i
    'Start building racks by outlining and filling in selected
    area
```

```
Selection.Borders(xlDiagonalDown).LineStyle = xlNone
Selection.Borders(xlDiagonalUp).LineStyle = xlNone
With Selection.Borders(xlEdgeLeft)
        .LineStyle = xlContinuous
        .Weight = xlThin
        .ColorIndex = xlAutomatic
End With
With Selection.Borders(xlEdgeTop)
        .LineStyle = xlContinuous
        .Weight = xlThin
        .ColorIndex = xlAutomatic
End With
With Selection.Borders(xlEdgeBottom)
        .LineStyle = xlContinuous
        .Weight = xlThin
        .ColorIndex = xlAutomatic
End With
With Selection.Borders(xlEdgeRight)
        .LineStyle = xlContinuous
        .Weight = xlThin
        .ColorIndex = xlAutomatic
End With
With Selection.Borders(xlInsideVertical)
        .LineStyle = xlContinuous
        .Weight = xlThin
        .ColorIndex = xlAutomatic
End With
With Selection.Borders(xlInsideHorizontal)
        .LineStyle = xlContinuous
        .Weight = xlThin
        .ColorIndex = xlAutomatic
End With
Range(Col_2 & Row_B).Select
Range_Select = ActiveWindow.RangeSelection.Address
Range(Col_1 & Row_A).Select
Row_Count = 2
If Row_B - Row_A > 1 Then
        Vertical = True
        'Vertical column of racks
        ActiveCell.Offset(0, 1).Select
```

'Eliminate every other line on right set of columns
Do
> *If ActiveWindow.RangeSelection.Address =*
> *Range_Select Then*
>> *Exit Do*
> *End If*
> *If Row_Count = 2 Then*
>> *Selection.Borders(xlEdgeLeft).LineStyle =*
>> *xlNone*
>> *Selection.Borders(xlEdgeBottom).LineStyle*
>> *= xlNone*
>> *Row_Count = 0*
> *End If*
> *ActiveCell.Offset(1, 0).Select*
> *Row_Count = Row_Count + 1*
> *Count = Count + 1*
> *If Count > 100 Then*
>> *Range(Col_1 & Row_A).Select*
>> *MsgBox ("Incorrect Rack width")*
>> *Exit Sub*
> *End If*
Loop
'If odd number of rows is selected eliminate odd row
If Row_Count = 2 Then
> *Selection.Borders(xlEdgeLeft).LineStyle = xlNone*
> *Selection.Borders(xlEdgeBottom).LineStyle =*
>> *xlNone*
> *Selection.Borders(xlEdgeRight).LineStyle = xlNone*
> *ActiveCell.Offset(0, -1).Select*
> *Selection.Borders(xlEdgeLeft).LineStyle = xlNone*
> *Selection.Borders(xlEdgeBottom).LineStyle =*
>> *xlNone*
>> *ActiveCell.Offset(0, 1).Select*
>> *ActiveCell.Offset(-1, 0).Select*
End If
ActiveCell.Offset(0, -1).Select
'Find top of column and return
Point_1 = ActiveWindow.RangeSelection.Address
Range(Col_1 & Row_A).Select

```
Range_Select =
ActiveWindow.RangeSelection.Address
Range(Point_1).Select
'Eliminate every other line on left set of columns
Row_Count = 2
Do
        If ActiveWindow.RangeSelection.Address =
        Range_Select Then
            Exit Do
        End If
        If Row_Count = 2 Then
            Selection.Borders(xlEdgeTop).LineStyle =
            xlNone
            Selection.Borders(xlEdgeRight).LineStyle =
            xlNone
            Row_Count = 0
        End If
        ActiveCell.Offset(-1, 0).Select
        Row_Count = Row_Count + 1
    Loop
Else:
    'Horizontal row of racks
    Horizontal = True
    ActiveCell.Offset(1, 0).Select
    'Eliminate every other line on bottom set of rows
    Do
        If ActiveWindow.RangeSelection.Address =
        Range_Select Then
            Exit Do
        End If
        If Row_Count = 2 Then
            Selection.Borders(xlEdgeRight).LineStyle =
            xlNone
            Selection.Borders(xlEdgeTop).LineStyle =
            xlNone
            Row_Count = 0
        End If
        ActiveCell.Offset(0, 1).Select
        Row_Count = Row_Count + 1
    Loop
```

'If odd number of rows is selected eliminate odd row
If Row_Count = 2 Then
    Selection.Borders(xlEdgeTop).LineStyle =
    xlNone
    Selection.Borders(xlEdgeBottom).LineStyle =
    xlNone
    Selection.Borders(xlEdgeRight).LineStyle =
    xlNone
    ActiveCell.Offset(-1, 0).Select
    Selection.Borders(xlEdgeRight).LineStyle =
    xlNone
    Selection.Borders(xlEdgeTop).LineStyle =
    xlNone
    ActiveCell.Offset(1, 0).Select
    ActiveCell.Offset(0, -1).Select
End If
ActiveCell.Offset(-1, 0).Select
'Find top of column and return
Point_1 = ActiveWindow.RangeSelection.Address
Range(Col_1 & Row_A).Select
Range_Select =
ActiveWindow.RangeSelection.Address
Range(Point_1).Select
'Eliminate every other line on left set of columns
Row_Count = 2
Do
    If ActiveWindow.RangeSelection.Address =
    Range_Select Then
        Exit Do
    End If
    If Row_Count = 2 Then
        Selection.Borders(xlEdgeBottom).LineStyle
        = xlNone
        Selection.Borders(xlEdgeLeft).LineStyle =
        xlNone
        Row_Count = 0
    End If
    ActiveCell.Offset(0, -1).Select
    Row_Count = Row_Count + 1
Loop

156

End If
ErrorHandler:
   Exit Sub
End Sub

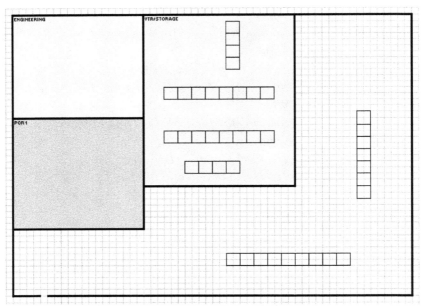

Here is an example of the result of the above code.

Sound and Video (PIZZAZZ Worksheet)

Play a Wave File

The wave file, or file with the .wav extension, contains digitized audio. The data within the file represents the sounds that you will hear when the file is played using any of the common media players. Any Windows computer contains many .wav audio files. To play this file type using VBA requires declaring the Windows MultiMedia .dll, and then band playing the .wav file using the function below.

The declaration appears as follows:

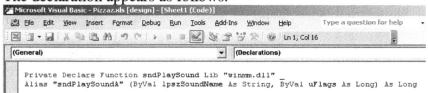

The function need only be declared once in the program for as many function calls to play the .wav file as you desire.

sndPlaySound "C:\windows\ringin.wav", 0

.

.

.

sndPlaySound "C:\myaudiofile.wav", 0

In the actual code it would look as follows:

```
Private Sub cmdPlayWaveFile_Click()
    'PLAY THE WAVE FILE
    sndPlaySound "C:\windows\ringin.wav", 0    'use your wave file path and name

End Sub
```

Notice that the *cmdPlayWaveFile_Click* is generated automatically when a control button is placed on the Excel spreadsheet.

158

Speak, Text to Voice

A computer running the Windows operating system has the ability to turn text into speech. It can read the text you place in the following command through your audio peripheral to the speakers.

```
Private Sub cmdSpeak_Click()

    Application.Speech.Speak "Help I'm trapped inside this computer"

End Sub
```

The default voice can be changed using the Control Panel. Go to Start→ Settings →Control Panel→ Speech as shown below.

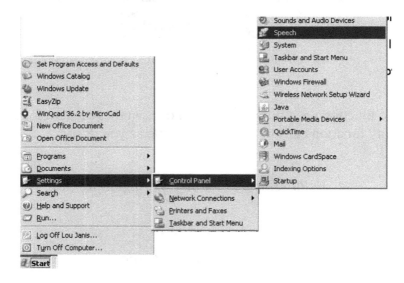

Select the *Text to Speech* tab, and then choose which voice you would like as the default.

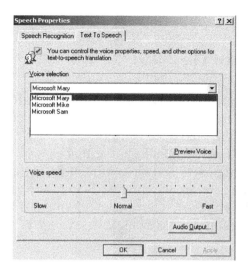

By pressing the Preview button, you can hear the voice you have selected. The voice speed may also be altered. Try different speeds and voices to determine the one you like best.

Play a MIDI File

MIDI files create music by specifying the characteristics of the instrument and how a note is played. Many MIDI files can be found on the Web, encompassing a full range of music.

```
Private Sub cmdPlayMidiFile_Click()

    'PLAY A MIDI FILE ON THE HARD DRIVE
    ret = mciSendString("open c:\midiPlay.mid type sequencer alias midi_Id", 0&, 0, 0) ' File path and name go here
    ret = mciSendString("play midi_Id wait", 0&, 0, 0)
    ret = mciSendString("close midi_Id", 0&, 0, 0)

End Sub
```

MIDI files have an extension of ".mid." This is different from the .wav files, which are digitized sound. MIDI files are more like sheet music; they are the instructions for the synthesizer software and sound card to follow in making music.

160

Create a MIDI File

The MIDI file format is available on the Web. It consists of a header, meta messages, and music tracks. The code we have included has only one track. Multitracks are normal in a more complex MIDI music file. To make this easy to understand, we have added comments and have limited the sample to three notes. The notes reference three cells in the spreadsheet so they may be easily changed. The numerical values that correspond to specific musical notes for a single octave are given below.

Note	Value
B	72
A	70
G	68
F	66
E	64
D	62
C	60

The values are in decimal, and the 60 refers to middle C. The code is as follows: starting by declaring variables (including an array of integers that is the data for the MIDI file.

```
Private Sub cmdPlayMusic_Click()
    '
    Dim music(68) As Byte
    Dim fileNum As Integer
    Dim x As Integer
    Dim index As Integer
    Dim ret As Long
    '
```

Next, the data making up the MIDI header are placed into the array.

```
' MAKE A MUSIC (MIDI) FILE
                'HEADER CHUNK
music(0) = 77    '-Chunk ID MThd
music(1) = 84    '
music(2) = 104   '
music(3) = 100   '
music(4) = 0     '-Chunk Size 00 00 00 06
music(5) = 0     '
music(6) = 0     '
music(7) = 6     '
music(8) = 0     '-Format Type 0 = 00 00
music(9) = 0     '
music(10) = 0    '-Number of Tracks is one = 00 01
music(11) = 1    '
music(12) = 0    '-Number of tick per quarter note = 128
music(13) = 128  '
```

At the beginning of the track information is the track identifier
and the length of the track. If you add or subtract notes, be sure
to recalculate the length of the track. Here is how to do the
calculation. Length = last location of the end footer – this
location. This location value is 21.

The indexes into the array will also have to be adjusted. The
array counts from zero to the last value in decimal.

```
                'TRACK CHUNK
music(14) = 77   '-Chunk ID MTrk
music(15) = 84   '
music(16) = 114  '
music(17) = 107  '
music(18) = 0    '-Chunk Size is a 4 byte binary value depending on the amount of data
music(19) = 0    '   this value will be filled in later
music(20) = 0    '
music(21) = 45   ' <<<<< very important to calculate the lenth correctly
                 '         length = last location of end footer - this location =  66 - 21 = 45
music(22) = 0    '-Delta Time to First MIDI Message in ticks
```

Next are the meta messages that set up various sound
characteristics.

```
                    'META MESSSAGES
                    '- #58 Meta Message
music(23) = 255     'FF
music(24) = 88      '58
music(25) = 4       '04
music(26) = 4       '04
music(27) = 2       '02
music(28) = 48      '30
music(29) = 8       '08
                    '
music(30) = 0       '-Delta Time to First MIDI Message in ticks
                    '- #59 Meta Message
music(31) = 255     'FF
music(32) = 89      '59
music(33) = 2       '02
music(34) = 0       '00
music(35) = 0       '00
                    '
music(36) = 0       '-Delta Time to First MIDI Message in ticks
```

Now play three notes. The value of each note is provided by the contents of a spreadsheet cell. This allows you to modify the values without changing the code. The way the cells are referenced is by using Range("cell location"). The cell location is a letter followed by a number.

Each note is played by pressing on a note with a velocity, like striking a key. This is followed by a delay and finally releasing the key.

163

```
                             'PLAY A NOTE
music(37) = 144 '90  Note ON
music(38) = Range("H3")  '60 = 3C = middle C
music(39) = 127 ' how hard you hit the key, with 00 for silent and 127 for very hard

music(40) = 129 '81 Time
music(41) = 0    '00

music(42) = 144 '90 Note OFF
music(43) = Range("H3")
music(44) = 0    '00

music(45) = 0    '-Delta Time to First MIDI Message in ticks

                             'PLAY A NOTE
music(46) = 144 '90
music(47) = Range("I3")
music(48) = 127 '

music(49) = 129 '81
music(50) = 0    '00          Notice the reference to a spreadsheet cell is how
                             the value is provided to the array
music(51) = 144 '90
music(52) = Range("I3")
music(53) = 0    '00

music(54) = 0    '-Delta Time to First MIDI Message in ticks

                             'PLAY A NOTE
music(55) = 144 '90
music(56) = Range("J3")
music(57) = 127 '

music(58) = 129 '81
music(59) = 0    '00

music(60) = 144 '90
music(61) = Range("J3")
music(62) = 0    '00

music(63) = 0    '-Delta Time to First MIDI Message in ticks
```

Finally, the track footer and since this has only one track, the end.

```
                    ' TRACK FOOTER
music(64) = 255 'FF
music(65) = 47  '2F
music(66) = 0    '00
```

At this point, we have an array of decimal values that represent the data in a MIDI file. To write it to the hard disk drive, proceed as follows.

```
'Write binary to file

Open "C:\midiPlay.mid" For Binary Access Write As FreeFile
Put #1, , music
Close #1
```

After writing the file to the hard disk drive, you may play it as follows.

```
'PLAY A MIDI FILE ON THE HARD DRIVE
   ret = mciSendString("open c:\midiPlay.mid type sequencer alias midi_Id", 0&, 0, 0)
   ret = mciSendString("play midi_Id wait", 0&, 0, 0)
   ret = mciSendString("close midi_Id", 0&, 0, 0)

End Sub
```

Display a Picture

From the toolbar select the Picture control by clicking on it then moving the pointer to the spreadsheet. Press and hold the left mouse button while dragging the mouse to the lower right; when the desired size picture box is reached, release the left mouse button.

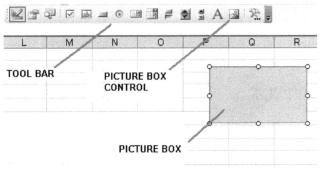

Next, right click inside the picture box.

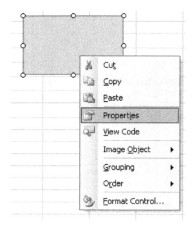

Select *Properties* and the Properties form will appear.

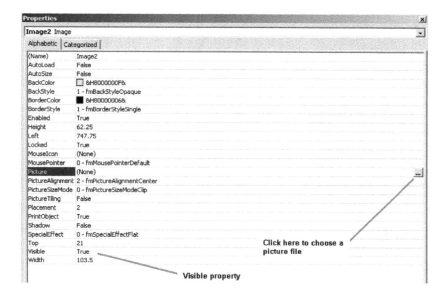

Click here to choose a picture file

Visible property

Clicking *choose a picture file to display* opens the following.

When you choose a picture file, its name will appear in the proper form and the file will appear in the picture box on the spreadsheet. If necessary, use the sizing handles to enlarge the box to fit the picture as shown.

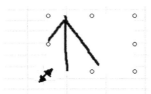

Drag the arrow to enlarge the picture box to fit the entire image.

Images added to the spreadsheet can be made visible under VBA code control.

```
Private Sub cmdMakePictureVisible_Click()

        Image2.Visible = True   ' NameOfControl.Property = True or False

End Sub
```

Or made invisible under VBA code control.

```
Private Sub cmdPictureInvisible_Click()

        Image2.Visible = False   ' NameOfControl.Property = True or False

End Sub
```

You can test the properties by directly changing the parameters in the properties form. This will display the valid parameters from which you may choose.

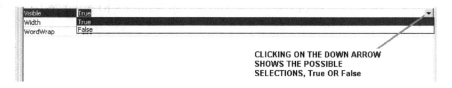

You will have to exit Design mode to see the picture change from visible to invisible as you run the VBA code or change properties manually.

Play a Video File

Audio-Video Interleave files have the extension .avi and are common on PCs running Microsoft Windows operating systems. Again, a command button is used to facilitate running the VBA code needed to play the .avi video file. After setting up the command button and finding an .avi file, the code is placed as shown.

```
Private Sub cmdPlayWindowVideo_Click()

    Dim CmdStr$                  ' Dim is used to declare a variable
                                 ' A variable name followed by $ is a string
    Dim ReturnVal&               ' A variable name followed by & is a long
                                 '    for now just a big binary number

    CmdStr$ = "play c:\globe.avi"
    ReturnVal& = mciSendString(CmdStr$, 0&, 0, 0&)

End Sub
```

A declaration to library functions is necessary to allow the .avi file to play on the PC. Library functions are used to extend the capabilities of a language so that every programmer doesn't need to recreate commonly used software routines.

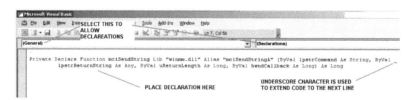

The function call passes several parameters to the library function. Some of the parameters are set to zero, while others may be missing. This indicates that there are other modes, values, or ways that the video file may be played. The code above plays the .avi file in a small window. The following code will play the image full screen.

```
Private Sub cmdFullScreenVideo_Click()
    Dim CmdStr$
    Dim ReturnVal&

    CmdStr$ = "play c:\globe.avi fullscreen "
    ReturnVal& = mciSendString(CmdStr$, 0&, 0, 0&)

End Sub
```

Learn more about VBA and libraries by searching the Web or using the VBA help.

Visual Basic for Applications provides an easy way to extend the capability of Microsoft Excel. With some variations, VBA is also useful in extending the capability of other Microsoft Office products. The event-driven, object-oriented techniques and basic constructs it uses are easily modified by those wanting to move to C++, C#, Java, or other programming languages. At this time, we have heard that VBA will continue on to new releases of the Microsoft Office product line, which means that the skills acquired via this book will be useful until the cows come home.